THOMASINA MIERS

MEXICAN FOOD

MADE SIMPLE

Photography by Tara Fisher

HODDER &
STOUGHTON

Thomasina Miers first arrived in Mexico aged 18, and fell so in love with its food that she went back to live there. She opened up a cocktail bar in Mexico City and used her free time to travel the country and cook with some of Mexico's top chefs. After returning to London and winning BBC2's *MasterChef* in 2005, Thomasina worked for six months with Skye Gyngell at Petersham Nurseries in Richmond, before opening the Mexican street food cantina, Wahaca, which promptly won the *Observer* Food Monthly's 'best cheap eats' award and, more recently, the London Food Festival's 'Discovery' award, 2009. Thomasina writes a regular recipe column for *The Times* and is co-editor of *Soup Kitchen* (2005) and the author of *Cook* (2006) and *Wild Gourmets* (2007).

First published in Great Britain in 2010 by Hodder & Stoughton
An Hachette UK company

2

A CIP catalogue record for this title is available from the British Library.

ISBN 978 0 340 99497 9

Designed by Ami Smithson at cabinlondon.co.uk

Typeset in Serifa by Bitstream and Old Claude by Adobe

Printed and bound in Great Britain by Butler Tanner & Dennis Ltd

Hodder & Stoughton policy is to use papers that are natural, renewable and recyclable products and made from wood grown in sustainable forests. The logging and manufacturing processes are expected to conform to the environmental regulations of the country of origin.

Hodder & Stoughton Ltd
338 Euston Road
London NW1 3BH

www.hodder.co.uk

To Alex, Sam and Damian who looked after me in Mexico,
and to Mark who found me when I came home

CONTENTS

Introduction

A land of food and flavour

Mexico – thousands of miles away, separated from us by the Atlantic Ocean and by an exciting but mysterious culture of salsa and chillies, wrestling, a bloodthirsty Aztec history and a passionate love for white corn. The country transfixed me when I stepped onto its soil for the first time and it still does today. It was so alive, so vivid with its music, its colour, its bustle and its chaotic sense of fun. I was 18 when I first arrived. I had barely left home before and was desperate for independence and thirsting for adventure. Mexico more than fulfilled my quest.

When I came home, I missed the colour and the people but in particular I yearned for the food. Everything about it had taken me by surprise. It was so full of intriguing flavours and spices, hot, refreshing and satisfying all at once.

In Mexican Food Made Simple, I will show you how easy, healthy and exciting Mexican food really is. I want to share the recipes that I have gathered over the years, their flavours far more familiar than you might expect, using ingredients that are all around you. And I will introduce you to the simple cooking techniques I have been shown by generous cooks and chefs.

The food I first tried in Mexico seemed exotic and out of reach, but the more I learn about this cuisine, the more I see the similarities in foods across the world. The first tamales I ate in Oaxaca strike me as a cross between Chinese dumplings and Italian polenta, the small corn parcels stuffed with sweet and savoury sauces and steamed in huge metal tins. In fact, many of the corn snacks sold from street stands in Mexico have parallels in the street food of the Far East and southern India.

As for taste, it is almost as if the British and the Mexicans were related in a former life. We share a love of slow-braised meats and an unadulterated passion for pork. Our food is rich with spices and allspice, clove, cinnamon and pepper also season Mexican sauces and marinades. We share a passion for puddings, whether it is for doughnuts (ours are filled with jam, theirs with toffee); rice pudding (in Mexico served chilled); custard or chocolate. We both love beer and drinking it with crispy, salty pork scratchings. We enjoy the occasional stiff drink, even if it's whisky here and tequila over there. We love having sauces and dressings with our food – ketchups, mayonnaises and jellies over here, salsas and moles over there.

You will find traces of Mexico all around you in your kitchen. Its amazing sunny climate has given us corn, avocados, courgettes and squash, tomatoes, chillies, chocolate, beans of all shapes and sizes, vanilla and coffee. Without Mexico, there would be no spaghetti Bolognese, no chocolate ice cream, no vanilla custard, no hot curries. Mexico's indigenous chillies, tomatoes and corn have travelled the world and put down roots in most other cuisines.

Simple techniques, lip-smacking flavours

In Mexico, cooks use a simple toolbox of flavourings to produce complex, rich dishes. Spices like cinnamon, allspice and cloves; herbs like coriander, bay leaves, thyme and oregano and fresh fruit and vegetables like lime, onion and chillies all infuse flavour into dishes using only one or two simple cooking techniques.

Freshly made or roast salsas appear in every cantina to spoon over your food, each with its own gentle, sweet, aromatic, citrusy or just ready to blow your head off character. They taste so different and the flavours are so complex, yet they are all made with just a few easy-to-learn cooking techniques.

First of all, fresh ingredients such as chillies, limes, herbs, tomatoes and fish are simply chopped up and served raw and fresh, packed with goodness and vitamins. For more complex flavours, onions, chillies and tomatoes are pan-roasted to add an extra depth. The same methods are used for making moles, just using more ingredients. Meats and seafood are marinated in a mix of chillies and citrus juices and then just grilled to add to tacos, tostadas and other street food. Alternatively, meats are left in the oven to slow-cook in spices and chilli marinades, then shredded and added to street food. In the same way as meat and fish are poached or marinated to add flavour, puddings are infused with flavours from vanilla pods and cinnamon sticks to star anise or citrus.

These simple cooking techniques are then complemented by a cuisine that embraces contrasts of texture, taste, colour and smell and has a neat way of building up flavour. Ingredients are layered over each other to create exotic-tasting dishes. Take any ingredient away and you are searching for the missing link, taste any flavour alone and you wonder what the fuss is about. The richness of cooked dishes is balanced by citrus juices and home-made vinegars, crunchy relishes and fresh salsas. Layer up a tostada, with the texture of crisp corn, the slow-cooked savoury filling, the crunch of fresh lettuce, the cool crema, the fire of a freshly made salsa and the tanginess of crumbled fresh cheese and you begin to get the ambrosial quality of Mexican food.

Let's bury that myth that associates Mexico with cheap, heavy food and discover what it's really about. Until the Spanish conquered Mexico, bringing with them the pig and sugar cane, the Aztecs lived largely off vegetables flavoured with spices and herbs. Gluten-free corn, protein-rich beans and chillies, tomatoes and courgettes, full of vitamins and minerals, formed the basis of their diet, with just the occasional turkey or goat to feast on if the hunters got lucky. Even the odd hot chocolate could not make inroads into this incredibly healthy diet.

Mexican food is a largely undiscovered cuisine that rivals the food of Italy, China, France or India. Over the centuries, the country's varied geography and many dialects separated its tribes and its hugely diverse and regional cuisine is the result of these barriers. A simple quesadilla will not only change its name, but its shape and the colour of its corn, depending on which region you are in, and even on which side of a particular river you happen to be. It's time to bring this great cuisine into your kitchen.

The Mexicans are a generous and food-loving race – use this book as a guide into their world and let their love affair with food capture your imagination.

The basics

Eating Mexican-style

What first intoxicated me about the culture in Mexico was the universal love of eating and sharing food that seemed to grip everyone, regardless of sex, age or class. There, the whole day is geared up to enjoying food, so if you are naturally greedy like me, you feel as if you have stumbled into paradise.

On my first visit to the country, we ate some of the best food I've ever tasted: from the light, ferociously fiery ceviches on the beaches as we lounged in hammocks reminiscing on the tequila-powered dancing of the night before, to vast amounts of salsa in the local taco stands and cantinas, simple corn snacks full of punch, rich, hearty stews and sharp, bright salads of radishes, onions and tomatoes.

I grew to love the deep, complex mole sauces flavoured with blends of chillies, nuts, spices and dried fruits. I savoured the spiced, fragrant hot chocolate, and the doughy pastries you dip into it, sweetened with locally harvested sugar cane molasses, anise syrups and wild honey. I developed a patriotic love for tequila and mescal.

Food in Mexico is all about these pleasures, about friends and families sharing plates of food and squabbling over favourite recipes. This is a country obsessed with good food!

Breakfast

Breakfast is a popular part of the day in Mexico, and with so many delicious treats on offer, it's easy to see why. Back in London, fried eggs on tortillas bathed in spicy tomato sauce (see page 172) or Mexican scrambled eggs (see page 174) make the perfect lazy weekend eating – and both beat the biggest of hangovers.

Midday snacks

When lunch isn't served 'til mid afternoon, it's impossible to resist snacking on antojitos [an-toh-hee-toss], the fresh, fast food sold at every corner taco stall in the country, designed to satisfy any craving.

Antojito translates literally as 'little whim', and whether it's tamales (light, fluffy, steamed corn dumplings) you fancy or a tasty soft tortilla stuffed, wrapped and topped with a plethora of fillings, Mexican street food is endlessly appealing.

I've included plenty of street food recipes in this book, because this is the food I love to eat and it is so easy to make at home. Find your favourite salsa (see Chapter 1) and try it on everything. Experiment with the recipes in Chapters 5 and 6 and work out if you like a dish in a taco, on a tostado or grilled and put in tortas and quesadillas.

A late lunch

At three, it's finally time for lunch. The food in Mexico is so regional that one cantina cooking Veracruzan food will be entirely different from another that does Yucatecan or Oaxacan specialities. What is always familiar though, is the pattern of eating lunch.

To start with, a plate of pickled vegetables or spicy roast nuts is put on the table, or we might choose a light ceviche or guacamole mashed with ripe, soft avocados. These light snacks and starters are a feast for the eyes and designed to get the appetite engaged.

Next up might be one of the soups that Mexico is justly famous for – all packed with flavour and delicious. Then some simply grilled fish or meat to share out and make into individual tacos, or slow-cooked meats made from cheap cuts and braised gently until falling apart. If you have room, there will be pudding, flavoured with the exotic fruits, vanilla beans and cocoa pods grown locally.

The Mexican lunch is so fluid and versatile that any part of it can be enjoyed as a feast for family and friends. Put down baskets of hot tortillas wrapped in napkins, and decorate your table with colourful bowls of fresh lime wedges, sour cream, chopped coriander and diced avocado. Add a few salsas to the table for ladling on flavour, colour, texture and spice. Serve with salad or moreish nibbles, like guacamole with chips or home-made pork scratchings (see Chapter 2), and follow up with something more substantial – fish or meat to throw on the grill or a slow-cooked joint that you put in the oven and forget about for a few hours (see Chapters 7 and 8). Fun, fantastic and full of flavour – this is food for people who love to eat.

The authentic ingredients?

People get caught up arguing about the authenticity of food, but spices and flavours have been travelling across the globe for centuries. Just as the Mexicans absorbed Spanish influences in their cuisine, I have no issue in recreating their food using whatever is available in our shops. I might not be able to buy Mexican corn here, but I can get hold of milled corn flour from Italy. I can't always get a good tortilla, but I can buy Middle Eastern flat breads and Indian chapattis.

And while I continue to search for Mexican chillies, I've found good substitutes among Indian, African and Spanish varieties. And thanks to global warming, the UK has the perfect climate to support chilli growth. It's never been easier to grow your own. What follows is my guide to cooking food that is distinctly Mexican in taste, character and nature without necessarily having all the right ingredients at your fingertips.

Corn and the tortilla

Under the Aztec ruler, Moctezuma, corn became a symbol of life and fertility and was offered up to the gods as a sacrifice (along with cacao and human beings!). These days, corn is still hugely important. Corn on the cob are sold all over the country, drizzled deliciously with cream and mayonnaise and then sprinkled with fresh lime, grated cheese and a touch of chilli powder. And corn dough, or 'masa', is used to make the Tortilla [tor-tee-ya].

Warm, soft and slightly charred, the tortilla is treated just like a chapatti or naan in India or the flat bread in Arabic and Asian cuisines – as the vehicle by which you carry food to your mouth. Filled and rolled around other goodies, tortillas become tacos.

Good corn tortillas are still hard to buy, so you can recreate the effect with flat breads from around the world, or make your own (see pages 100 and 101). In the north of Mexico, home of the burrito, wheat is a more popular crop,

so wheat flour tortillas often take the place of corn ones and are available in shops across this country. Look for the thinnest ones you can find – often Middle Eastern and Indian flat breads are better quality than the thick flour tortillas sold in the Tex-Mex aisles.

Chillies

When I first travelled to Mexico, I was under the impression that chillies were red or green and either hot or damned hot. Instead I found dozens of different varieties, both fresh and dried, piled up in big sacks in the markets and with a dizzying collection of exotic names, shapes and sizes. Reddish chillies, I discovered, are a bit riper than green, but they are interchangeable in recipes.

I came to realise that when talking about chillies, there was a whole new language that needed to be learnt. The chillies I tried were earthy, sweet, spicy and complex, with emerging notes of molasses, tobacco, grass, citrus and chocolate. The incredible range of flavours

means that some are more suited to rich braises, some fresher ones are perfect for salsas and others complement particular foods like mushrooms (the pasilla), seafood (the ancho) and cheese (the jalapeño).

Exotic varieties of chillies are increasingly dried and sold over here, giving a much wider palate of chillies to play with. Dried chillies also often have a meaty, earthy flavour that you can't get from fresh. In the same way you would soften dried porcini to capture their incredible flavour, soak dried chillies for about 15 minutes to release the flavours of the Mexican sunshine.

The heat varies in every chilli, so if you want to know more or less how hot a fresh chilli is, just cut a tiny slice from the bottom and touch it to your tongue. The average supermarket chilli is not very hot, although a few varieties like the habanero or Scotch bonnet and the tiny green bird's eye chillies are almost always blistering. The heat of chillies is most intense at the stem and in the membranes where the seeds are attached. If you want a little less heat, remove all the seeds and membranes before cooking with the chilli flesh.

One last thing, always wash your hands thoroughly after handling chillies and scrub them after handling the hot ones. Try not to rub your eyes whilst using them or go to the loo, as it can have painful results!

Beans

Beans are vital to this cuisine, and Mexicans enjoy a staggering variety, including types of creamy borlotti and cranberry, nutty chickpeas, rattlesnake and turtle. The most widely used beans tend to be earthy black and rich pinto varieties, which are readily available over here, and also fresh borlotti beans, which are particularly good in salads. Beans are traditionally served whole, cooked in water with aromatic herbs and vegetables (see page 62), or refried (see page 63) in oil or lard with onions and garlic. I particularly adore the flavour of black beans, which you can now buy dried or cooked in tins or cartons in most UK supermarkets.

Rice

Rice provides a complex carbohydrate in the Mexican diet. Rice is long-grain in Mexico and usually cooked in a broth flavoured with coriander and greens or tomatoes and other vegetables (see page 64). The cooking is normally finished in the oven where the rice is allowed to steam for half an hour before eating. Mexican rice is light, fluffy and nutty with a delicate bite to it. I use basmati rice, which is an excellent substitute.

Herbs

Herbs are used in Mexican recipes to add flavour to soups, salsas, stocks, stews, beans and sauces. The ones I use most in Mexican cookery are coriander, mint, parsley and thyme (all widely available in the supermarkets), together with fresh oregano, which you can grow yourself. Dried oregano is also commonly used in Mexico, although they have a much more aromatic variety over there, so either up the amount called for in the recipe or buy the dried Mexican variety (see Suppliers list, page 218).

Some Mexican herbs are harder to find over here. Hoja santa, for instance, is a large-leafed plant that grows all over Mexico and has a subtle anise flavour. It is used to cook eggs, fish and other delicate-tasting food. I have found that a combination of chervil, tarragon and bay mimics it well or substitute ⅛ teaspoon ground anise for 1 leaf of hoja santa. Epazote is a strange-tasting herb used to flavour soups, stews and beans as we use the bay leaf. Whilst it is grown here in the summer, it is largely only available in dry form from specialist suppliers. When I cook beans, I sometimes add anise seeds or star anise in place of epazote.

Try growing your own herbs in pots at home and if you have any outside space, buy a bay tree so that you always have access to the fresh leaves.

Spices

The Mexicans use an enormous variety of spices to flavour their soups, stocks and marinades. The most commonly used ones include allspice, a berry originally from Mexico with a slightly sweet, rounded flavour, and cloves, which have a strong aromatic flavour – use sparingly. Cinnamon sticks are used more often than ground cinnamon because their flavour is subtler and gently sweet and aromatic; star anise and pepper are also frequently used. All these spices can be found whole or ground in most supermarkets and delicatessens across the UK.

I like to grind all my spices in a pestle and mortar or spice grinder as this keeps the flavours very fresh. For seasoning, I always use flaky sea salt and freshly ground black pepper.

Vinegar

Home-made vinegars are very popular in Mexico and are both cheap and easy to make. Favourites are made from pineapples, guavas and apples and all have a characteristically soft, sweet tartness to them with none of the astringency of mass-produced vinegar. A good balsamic vinegar tastes similar to a matured fruit vinegar. Aspall cider vinegar is my personal favourite.

Tomatillos

Tomatillos are related to the cape gooseberry and have a delicious tart and citrusy flavour. They are hard to get over here so I have only included them in one recipe in this book, but if you are very keen, bug your local shop to stock them or see Suppliers list on page 218.

Tomatillos are used for Mexico's most popular table salsa, salsa verde, a vivid green, fiery hot salsa made from serrano chillies, tomatillos, onions, garlic, coriander and fresh lime.

Avocados

Hass are generally the avocado to choose when out shopping because they have a lovely creamy flesh – yet another example of something that is both delicious and good for you. A ripe avocado should have firm, but yielding flesh that gives a little when pressed. The pip at the tip should come away easily.

Most supermarkets store avocados in cool temperatures and they are rock hard when you buy them. In this case, store them in brown paper bags somewhere warm like an airing cupboard or on a windowsill that gets lots of sun. Putting a banana in with the avocados ripens them all the more quickly. On no account keep them in the fridge. And don't bother using an avocado if it isn't ripe – it is just not worth it.

Lard

No Mexican would cook without it, but if you shudder at the thought of lard, butter, vegetable oil or olive oil can be used instead.

Meat

In Mexico, thriftiness in the kitchen is not a fashion, it is de rigueur, and housewives would think it insanity to throw food out until the maximum amount of flavour had been extracted from it. Before the Spanish conquered Mexico, very little meat was eaten, so when the Spanish arrived with the pig, and later cattle were reared, meat was seen as a real treat. That mentality of thinking of meat as a luxury item has still survived today. It is totally normal to use every single part of an animal in recipes, the bones are always made into stock and leftovers celebrated and used to make feasts for the next day. Cheap

cuts of beef and lamb are often favoured over more expensive ones, whether it is a shoulder or brisket for slow-cooking and shredding or skirt steak for flash grilling, all are used to stuff inside the various street food snacks. Flavour stands for everything.

Chorizo

Chorizo crops up a lot in Mexican cooking, thanks to the Spanish invasion and the arrival of the pig. The main difference between Mexican and Spanish chorizo (apart from a few spices) is that in Mexico it is always sold in the form of a sausage, for cooking. Nowadays, cooking chorizo is much more widely available in supermarkets and delicatessens, so do try to buy it instead of the more commonly found chorizo salami.

Fish

Mexico has a rich source of seafood thanks to its enormous coastline. Prawns, scallops, king prawns and lobster vie for attention with kingfish, red snapper, tuna and cod. However, just as I think it would be mad only to use Mexican pork or beef in Mexican recipes, I similarly do not think it logical to use Mexican fish in its seafood recipes. Wherever possible in this book, I use sustainable species of fish whose stocks are not in huge decline (see www.fishonline.org for advice).

Cheeses and creams

With their fresh curd cheeses, melting string cheeses, goat's and cream cheeses, the dairy stands in Mexican markets are an impressive sight. When you consider that, for centuries, the diet of the Mexican Indians consisted largely of vegetables and corn, it is not surprising that dairy became so important in their cuisine. There is a huge choice of cheeses and creams available over there and each type of cheese has its different use in the kitchen. Luckily, dairy is an equally important part of our food culture and I have learnt that many of the cheeses we can buy here have very similar flavour profiles to Mexican ones. See a list of Mexican cheeses and their western counterparts on page 123.

Mexican crema is a slightly soured cream with the ability to melt smoothly into soup without separating. It is used throughout Mexican cooking to add a creaminess that softens the heat of the bright, fiery salsas. Crema is thicker and creamier than crème fraîche, but lighter than sour cream. Either can be used as an alternative, though as a rule sour cream works better with hot food.

Sugar

The Mexicans have a sweet tooth and most puddings are traditionally sweetened with either the dark, rich flavours of unrefined sugar cane called piloncillo, or with agave syrup extracted from cactus. The latter is an incredibly healthy, low-GI product sold in supermarkets and health food shops throughout the UK. If I can't get hold of piloncillo, I use a dark demerara or muscovado sugar, or even Indian jaggery, to get the sweet, nutty flavour of unrefined sugar.

Vanilla

Vanilla has a haunting, elusive flavour that I find irresistible. It makes the most delicious puddings: heated up and infused in creams, chocolate sauces, ice creams and fruit puddings. In Mexico, they even add it to strong red wine sauces to serve with beef. Vanilla pods are indigenous to the forests of Veracruz in Mexico. After the Spanish conquest, it was taken to Madagascar and Tahiti by traders, where it is grown today, although aficionados still think the best vanilla comes from Mexico. The pods are normally poached in liquid and then cut down the middle so that the seeds can be scraped out and put into the dish. The flavour is delicious with poached fruit.

Chocolate

Revered in Mexico since the Aztecs, chocolate is spiced with cinnamon, all spice or cloves, and sometimes even a touch of chilli, and traditionally used to flavour either sweet or savoury dishes. Try to find at least 70% cocoa solids when you are buying chocolate for cooking.

Tequila

Tequila impostors are made up with nasty additives and chemicals that make you feel grim the morning after. Real tequila, on the other hand, is made with 100% blue agave, a plant that grows for 10 to 12 years in the hot Mexican sun before it is harvested. All these years of sunshine create an enormous amount of sugar, which is distilled to tequila.

Blanco tequila is young tequila bottled as soon as it is distilled with the distinctive, herbaceous flavour of the agave plant. Reposado tequila has been aged between 2 and 12 months in oak barrels and has a mellower flavour with notes of vanilla and honey. Añejo tequila is aged between 1 and 3 years and can be sipped like Cognac after dinner. It has an extremely smooth flavour. I cook a lot with blanco tequila for its fresh agave flavour and occasionally with reposado tequila.

I have discovered over the years that tequila makes me feel happy and my theory, though not corroborated, is that anything that has been bathing in the sun for quite so long will be full of good solar energy and therefore bound to put a smile on your face. Go and buy some of the real stuff at the next available opportunity, and see what it does for you.

CHAPTER I

Salsas, sauces & relishes

If, like me, you love ketchup, chutneys, mustards and pickles, then you might become addicted to the salsas, sauces and relishes in this chapter.

Mexican **salsas** are quick and easy to make and add a splash of fire and flavour to everything you dollop them on. Fresh table salsas are made up of simply chopped raw ingredients, mixed with brightly flavoured vinegars or lime juice. Or you can make roast salsas for extra punch and these are huge fun to cook. Throwing onions, garlic and chillies onto a dry frying pan takes no effort, but you will feel like you are really cooking the Mexican way.

Relishes are just like salsas in that they are placed on the table to add flavour to whatever you're eating. The only difference is that vinegar or lime juice is used to soften and cure the ingredients in them, so they need a little time to marinate.

Sauces in Mexico are called moles [moll-ays] (hence 'Guacamole', the classic avocado sauce), and are normally cooked more slowly than a salsa blending ingredients like chillies, chocolate, nuts, spices and dried fruit. The traditional mole can look like a serious commitment, with its long list of ingredients and elaborate cooking steps, but start with a simple recipe (see pages 42 and 43), poured over shredded meat or fish or spooned on to grills, and you'll soon understand why these sauces play a starring role in Mexican cooking.

Chillies are the essential ingredient in all these recipes. There are over 200 varieties of Mexican chillies, with each region in Mexico growing its own to use fresh or dried. Few of these are available in the UK, but the six listed overleaf are my tried and tested favourites – each with unique flavour and heat, and increasingly easy to buy here.

Chipotle (heat rating 7/10)

A chipotle is a smoked, dried jalapeño chilli, about the size of a prune with an intoxicating fiery flavour. Sold dried or in a sweet-spiced sauce, called an 'adobo', it adds enormous flavour to braised meats, sauces and dressings.

Chile de árbol (heat rating 9/10)

The original red, hot chilli pepper, the chile de árbol scatters an addictive sprinkling of fire over anything it touches. You can use pepperoncino, the small Italian dried chilli, as a substitute or dried chilli flakes.

Ancho chilli (heat rating 3/10)

Sweet, fat, round and mild, when soaked in water and puréed, this chilli adds an incredible sweetness and depth of flavour to meat marinades and salsas. If you can't find an ancho chilli, substitute with Spanish dried red peppers.

Serrano (heat rating 8/10)

Smaller and skinnier than the jalapeño, serranos have a fresh, grassy, hot flavour and are used finely chopped or puréed in vibrant fresh table salsas. Grow your own with Wahaca's giveaway chilli seeds, or substitute with any fresh green chilli.

Jalapeño (heat rating 7/10)

Green, curvy, fresh and spicy, these fiery chillies can pack quite a punch, although the heat won't last long (and can vary hugely from one chilli to another). Substitute with any fresh green chilli or add a few tiny bird's eye chillies for a proper tongue tingle.

Habanero (heat rating 10/10)

Habaneros, aka Scotch bonnets, look like brightly coloured Chinese lanterns. Beneath this attractive exterior lies a delicious fruity flavour, and a menacing heat that is liable to blow your head off.

Fresh tomato salsa

Enough for 6–8 people

Preparation time:
15 minutes

8 very ripe plum tomatoes
a small handful of
    coriander, stalks removed
    and roughly chopped
1 small red onion,
    very finely diced
2 jalapeño chillies,
    very finely chopped
1 tablespoon extra virgin
    olive oil
1–2 limes, freshly squeezed
1 teaspoon soft brown
    or demerara sugar
1 tablespoon sea salt
black pepper

This salsa is lightly fiery and delicious before supper with tortilla chips (see page 113); mixed with black beans; on grilled steaks and chicken and lots more besides. Make it with summer's ripe tomatoes and use a really good extra virgin olive oil.

Cut the tomatoes into quarters and remove the insides because these will make the salsa watery (you can keep them and use them to make a tomato sauce). Dice the flesh.

Stir the coriander into the tomatoes with the onion, chillies, olive oil, half the lime juice and the sugar, salt and pepper. Check the flavour and add more salt, pepper or lime juice if you think the salsa needs it. Leave to marinate for at least 20 minutes before you are ready to eat.

Searingly hot salsa

Makes about a cup

Cooking time:
10 minutes

40g small chiles de arbol
250ml cider vinegar
    (or a mix of white wine
    and rice vinegar)
1 teaspoon dried oregano
4 cloves of garlic,
    roughly chopped
1 teaspoon peppercorns
2 teaspoons sea salt
a couple of good pinches
    of caster sugar

This salsa makes a beautiful counterpoint to the meatiness of the rich lamb barbacoa on page 146 or any other slow-braised meat. Drizzle on as much as you dare. This is the table salsa for anyone addicted to chillies.

Remove the stems from the chillies and simmer the chillies in 100ml water for 5 minutes. Whiz up in a blender with all the other ingredients. Serve (in moderation) with anything you fancy.

Store in a clean, sterilized jar in the refrigerator. The salsa will keep for a few weeks.

Sweetcorn &
black bean salsa

You can ladle this onto anything from barbecued chicken to steak, sausages and salads or use as a filling for jacket potatoes with plenty of butter and Cheddar cheese.

First make the dressing. Bash the garlic, chilli, salt and cumin in a pestle and mortar until the garlic is completely crushed and then add the lime juice, olive oil and pepper.

Simmer the corn for about 5 minutes in a small pan of salted water until the kernels are tender. Shave them off the cob with a knife and dress whilst still warm. Add the rest of the ingredients and season to taste.

Makes about a cup

Preparation time:
20 minutes

For the dressing
1 clove of garlic
½ jalapeño chilli, chopped
a few teaspoons sea salt
a generous pinch of
    ground cumin
juice of ½ lime
2 tablespoons very good
    quality extra virgin olive oil
generous amount of
    black pepper

For the salsa
1 corn on the cob
100g cooked black beans
    (see page 62)
4 spring onions, finely sliced
3 plum tomatoes, peeled, de-
    seeded and roughly diced
a small handful of coriander
    leaves, roughly chopped
1½ jalapeño chillies,
    finely chopped

Step 1. Gather together all of your ingredients and heat a large, heavy-bottomed frying pan over a high heat.

Step 2. Place the tomatoes, garlic and chilli in the dry frying pan and dry roast until they are blackened, blistered and soft. The tomatoes will take a little longer, so remove the garlic and chilli first as they are cooked (about 5 to 10 minutes).

A simple roast chilli salsa

This is a quick and easy table salsa, the likes of which grace every cantina across Mexico, and it goes with anything. Once you have a feel for how to roast vegetables in a dry frying pan, start experimenting with different chillies.

Makes about a cup
Cooking time: 20 minutes

4 plum tomatoes
2 cloves of garlic, unpeeled
1 large jalapeño chilli

1 large tablespoon chopped
  coriander
½ white onion, finely chopped
  and rinsed under cold water
juice of ½ lime
a pinch of sea salt

NOTE This can all be done in a food processor, but you will lose the lovely rough consistency that you get with the pestle and mortar.

Step 3. Remove and discard the stem from the chilli and the skin from the garlic and put both in a pestle and mortar. Pound to a paste, then add the tomatoes and work them into the chilli.

Step 4. Add the coriander, onion and lime juice. Taste and check for seasoning.

Roast chipotle salsa

Omit the jalapeño and raw white onion and roast an onion, chopped in quarters, along with the garlic and tomatoes. Blend in a food processor with a Chipotles en adobo (see page 36), seasoning with lime juice, coriander and salt as above.

Classic roast salsa verde

Roast 500g tomatillos in place of the tomatoes (or if you can't get them, use green tomatoes) and 2 serrano chillies in place of the jalapeño. Prepare as above.

A blow-your-head-off salsa

Makes about a cup

Cooking time:
20–25 minutes

2 tablespoons vegetable
    or olive oil
1 medium onion, chopped
2 cloves of garlic, chopped
3 carrots, diced into
    small cubes
1 teaspoon freshly ground
    coriander
500ml water
2 habaneros (Scotch bonnets)
    stems removed
200ml white wine vinegar or
    good quality cider vinegar
a heaped teaspoon honey
1 tablespoon sea salt
½ teaspoon dried oregano
    or 1 teaspoon of fresh
    if available

This is the most delicious hot sauce. If you are not mad on heat use one habanero instead of two – you can always add more later. I love this salsa on the barbequed monkfish tail on page 161, and spooned over refried beans. It takes very little time to make and all the ingredients can be found in supermarkets.

Heat the oil in a pan and sweat the onion and carrots for 10 minutes before adding the garlic and coriander. Cook until the onion turns translucent and then add the water. Bring to a boil and simmer until the carrots are soft. Add the remaining ingredients and purée in a blender until smooth.

Store in a clean sterilized jar in the refrigerator.

NOTE If you use dried oregano make sure it has not been lurking in your cupboard for too long or it tends to taste a bit musty.

Roast tomato sauce

Makes enough for 4–6

Cooking time:
40 minutes

12 large ripe, sweet
    tomatoes
1 onion, quartered
2 jalapeño chillies
3 cloves of garlic
olive oil
sea salt and black pepper
a good splash of red
    wine vinegar
a bay leaf

This spicy tomato sauce gets its flavour from the herbs and from the simple way the tomatoes and chillies are roasted in a dry frying pan, Mexican style (see page 28). For a milder sauce, cut down on the chilli or just take out the seeds. This is a sauce for cooking with, not a table salsa, and is great to use on eggs, over enchiladas, such as the Spinach and ricotta enchiladas on page 184, or in the Chicken and corn humble pie (see page 175).

Roast the tomatoes, onion, chillies and garlic in a large, dry frying pan until they are blistered, blackened and softened all over. The garlic and chillies will be ready at least 5 minutes before the onion and tomatoes, so remove them as they are cooked. Cool slightly, then peel away the skin from all the vegetables, remove the seeds from the chilli if you wish, and roughly purée the vegetables in a food processor.

In a large, heavy-bottomed saucepan, heat 2 tablespoons olive oil and add the puréed sauce, cooking for a few minutes over a high heat. Turn the heat right down and season generously with salt and pepper, the vinegar and bay leaf. Simmer gently for 15 to 20 minutes, stirring regularly, until the mixture has reduced and slightly thickened. Add the chopped herbs and sugar and check the seasoning.

This sauce will keep well for several days in the fridge and it also freezes well.

1 small handful of tarragon, chopped

1–2 tablespoons chervil, chopped

a pinch of demerara sugar (optional)

Tangy olive & caper tomato sauce

Makes enough for 4

This is a classic tomato sauce that is served in Veracruz with baked or grilled fish (see page 165) or mixed with prawns and other shellfish to spoon over tostadas. It is thought that the flavours were brought to Veracruz by the Spanish, with strong influences from Sicily. For a simpler sauce, leave out the spices.

Cover the tomatoes with boiling water and count to 20. Drain and pierce them with a knife so that the skins slip off easily. Dice into small cubes.

Heat the olive oil in a pan and sauté the shallots until translucent. Add the garlic, chillies, bay, thyme and oregano and sauté for another few minutes. Add the diced tomato, olives, capers, cinnamon and allspice and cook for another 10 minutes until the tomato has dissolved a little into the sauce. Season with salt, pepper and perhaps a pinch of sugar if the tomatoes were not too ripe. Stir in the fresh parsley and mint.

Winter tomato salsa

In the winter, use two 400g tins of plum tomatoes instead of fresh and simmer the sauce for at least 20 minutes for the flavours to deepen. This is delicious with rich food like duck and partridge.

Cooking time:
25 minutes

10 large plum tomatoes

1–2 tablespoons olive oil

3 shallots, finely chopped

3 cloves of garlic, sliced

4 pickled jalapeños, chopped

2 bay leaves, preferably fresh

1 tablespoon each of thyme and oregano leaves, roughly chopped

10 large pimiento-stuffed green olives

2 tablespoons capers (preferably salted ones, rinsed)

1 cinnamon stick

½ teaspoon ground allspice

sea salt and black pepper

a small handful each of chopped parsley and mint

Smoky tomato sauce

Makes enough for 6

Cooking time:
as slow as you can

2 x 400g tins plum tomatoes
   or 700g very ripe
   tomatoes
olive oil or lard
1 onion, finely sliced
2 cloves of garlic, crushed
¼ teaspoon ground
   cumin
sea salt and black pepper
150ml medium-bodied
   red wine
1 bay leaf
4–5 sprigs of thyme or
   oregano
a pinch of demerara sugar
1–2 tablespoons Chipotle
   purée (see page 37)
300ml water or chicken or
   vegetable stock (fresh
   or cube)

This is a rich, deep, sweet and spicy sauce with the smoky flavour of chipotle chillies giving it its character. The slower you cook this, the more richly flavoured it will be. It can sit happily on a very low heat while you get on with something else and it freezes beautifully. Brilliant with enchiladas or the Meatballs de Mehico! (see page 143).

If you are using fresh tomatoes, cover the tomatoes with boiling water and count to 20. Drain and pierce them with a knife so that the skins slip off easily.

Heat a couple of tablespoons of olive oil or lard in a large, heavy-bottomed pan and when it is gently sizzling, add the onion and cook for at least 5 minutes until the onion is softening and turning translucent. You can cook the onion for anything from 5 to 30 minutes, but the longer it cooks, the sweeter the tomato sauce will be.

Add the garlic and cumin and continue cooking for a few minutes more, seasoning well with salt and pepper. Before the onion starts to colour, add the wine, herbs, tomatoes and sugar. Spoon in the chipotle purée, a little at a time if you are not mad on very hot food (you can always add more later if you want to ramp it up) and cook for 5 minutes, breaking up the tomatoes with a wooden spoon.

Add the water or stock and simmer gently until you have a rich tomato sauce, about 15 to 20 minutes. Check for seasoning.

Diana's delicious meat marinade

Makes enough for 6–8

My Mexican friend and mentor Diana Kennedy taught me this recipe. Rich, warming and packed full of flavour, it is used in the wonderful Barbacoa (see page 146) and is also incredible on lamb, mutton and beef. Marinate cheap cuts like shoulder, shin, brisket or neck end overnight and then braise and you will be able to feed a lot of people for not a lot of money.

Tear out the stems from the chillies and discard the seeds. Tear the flesh into a few flattish pieces.

Warm a dry frying pan and, when medium-hot, gently heat the chilli pieces for about 10 to 20 seconds, turning to heat on both sides. Be careful not to burn them. The heat brings out the flavour of the chillies (as you would warm spices before grinding them) and they are ready when you can smell the oils from the chillies and the skin starts to soften.

Put the chillies in a small saucepan, cover with boiling water and simmer for 10 to 15 minutes until soft. Blend them in an upright blender with about a third of the soaking water or until just smooth. Add the spices, garlic, oregano and chocolate to the blender and purée with the olive oil. Season well with salt and pepper.

This marinade keeps for up to a fortnight in the fridge and freezes well.

NOTE If you are short of time you can skip out the toasting step and just simmer the pieces in boiling water until soft.

Cooking time:
15–20 minutes

5 ancho chillies
8 cloves of garlic, roughly chopped
1 cinnamon stick, broken up
$\frac{2}{3}$ teaspoon cumin seeds
$\frac{1}{2}$ teaspoon peppercorns
1 teaspoon dried oregano
40g dark chocolate (70% cocoa solids), broken up
300ml olive oil
sea salt and black pepper

Pink pickled onions

Makes about a cup

Preparation time:
10 minutes +
2 hours marinating

2 red onions, thinly sliced
juice of 1 orange
juice of 2 limes
1 habanero (Scotch bonnet)
    chilli, very finely chopped
sea salt and black pepper
a small handful of
    coriander leaves, chopped

This relish is a brilliant neon pink colour and is used to decorate and flavour dishes across the Yucatán region of Mexico. It adds a citrusy vibrancy to food and is particularly good on top of slow-cooked pork, grilled chicken or as a colourful topping for black beans.

Cover the onion slices with boiling water and soak for 10 minutes. Drain and then add the orange and lime juices and chilli.

Season well with salt and pepper and, using your hands, scrunch up the chilli in the marinade and leave to marinate for several hours, washing your hands meticulously afterwards. Scatter with chopped coriander when serving.

This relish will keep well for several days in the fridge.

Chopped chilli relish

Makes 2 jam jars full

Preparation time:
35 minutes +
overnight marinating

15 ancho chillies
6 baby shallots,
    very finely chopped
6 cloves of garlic,
    finely chopped
50ml good-quality
    red wine vinegar
80ml rice wine vinegar
2 teaspoons thyme leaves
200ml extra virgin olive oil
    plus extra for drizzling

To serve
grated Pecorino or
    Lancashire cheese

This is the most delicious relish and all you have to do is chop the ingredients into small pieces and leave them to steep in the olive oil and vinegar. A few hours later, you'll have a brilliant accompaniment for grilled or roast meats that lasts for months in the fridge. It is yummy dolloped over the Black bean, tomato & feta tostadas on page 116.

Wipe the chillies clean with a damp cloth and then break them open, discarding the stems and seeds. Using a large, very sharp chopping knife or a pair of scissors, cut the chillies up into small shreds. Mix them into the shallots, garlic, vinegars, thyme and olive oil and season generously with salt and pepper.

Put in the fridge to allow the flavours to develop for at least a few hours, but preferably overnight so that the chillies have a chance to soften.

Stir before serving, pour over a drizzle of extra virgin olive oil and sprinkle with a little grated Pecorino or Lancashire cheese.

Step 1. Wash the chipotles in cold water and drain. Snip off the stalk end of each chilli with scissors, which will allow the water to penetrate their tough skins.

Step 2. Cover the chillies with water in a medium pan and simmer for 30 to 40 minutes until completely soft. When the chillies are soft, rinse off any excess seeds.

Chipotles en adobo

This smoky, slightly sweet purée harnesses the intense flavours of dried chipotle chillies, lasts for months, and is an indispensable ingredient in my kitchen. A small teaspoon is delicious stirred into stews, pasta sauces, dressings and mayonnaises.

Makes about a litre
Cooking time:
1 hour

200g chipotle chillies (about 65)
1 large white onion, roughly chopped
a head of garlic, cloves roughly chopped
3 tablespoons fresh oregano leaves or a few good pinches of dried oregano

1–2 tablespoons thyme leaves
2 fresh bay leaves
1 teaspoon cumin seeds, crushed
4 tablespoons olive oil
350ml good-quality white wine vinegar
50ml good-quality balsamic vinegar
3 tablespoons tomato purée
7 tablespoons demerara or palm sugar
2 tablespoons sea salt

Step 3. Put the onion, garlic, herbs and cumin into a blender (or a stick blender is just as easy) with 200ml water and six of the chillies. Purée to a smooth paste.

Step 4. Heat the olive oil in a large, heavy-bottomed pan until it is smoking hot. Add the chilli paste and fry for about 3 minutes, stirring continuously with a spatula to prevent it catching and burning. Add the vinegars, tomato purée, sugar, salt and another 100ml water and cook for 5 more minutes before adding the rest of the chillies. Cook, whilst stirring, for a further 15 minutes and at the end check to see if the purée needs more salt or sugar. Store in clean, sterilised jam or Kilner jars.

NOTE I often blend the chipotles into a purée after they are cooked, which makes them easier to measure out into recipes. If not, just finely chop before adding to recipes, or break them up with a wooden spoon.

My addictive sweet chipotle paste

Makes about a small cup

Preparation time:
10 minutes

3 cloves of garlic
5 Chipotles en adobo (see page 36)
3 tablespoons demerara sugar
juice and zest of 1 lime
2 teaspoons fish sauce
sea salt and black pepper

This is the yummiest sauce to spoon over pasta, prawns or crab, before or after cooking, or to mix into a dressing. Try smearing it on chicken wings and barbecuing them or serve with the spicy crab noodles on page 178. I guess it is the Mexican equivalent of a sweet chilli sauce. I love it in sandwiches. I love it on anything.

To make the paste, bash the cloves of garlic with the Chipotles and sugar in a pestle and mortar or with a rolling pin until they are a paste. Add the lime and fish sauce and season with plenty of black pepper and a little sea salt and check for seasoning.

The paste should be spicy and sweet, salty, fresh and zesty. Add more sugar, lime or fish sauce if you are not immediately addicted to the flavour. When you hit the right balance, you will know by the compulsive way your spoon keeps going back into the bowl to check for seasoning.

WHY NOT TRY
Mix an equal quantity of this paste with unsalted butter. Make a watercress salad, grill a piece of skirt steak and add a slice of this chipotle butter to the steak the second it is off the griddle.

Chipotle mayonnaise

Makes a large cup

Preparation time:
15 mins

3 egg yolks
5 teaspoons of Dijon mustard
2 Chipotles en adobo (see page 36)
sea salt and black pepper
juice and zest of 1 lime
2 cloves of garlic, crushed
100ml olive oil

This chilli mayonnaise will liven up any sandwich. It is particularly great in a Mexican club sandwich (see page 156) or served alongside deep-fried fish.

To make the mayonnaise, put the egg yolks in a food processor with the mustard, half the Chipotles, a good pinch of salt and the garlic and whiz to combine.

With the motor running, slowly drip the oil through the funnel of the food processor until the mayonnaise starts to thicken and emulsify, at which time you can pour in the oil in a thin stream.

Add half the vinegar and the sugar and taste (it may not need the other half). Season and add more chipotle if you like the mayonnaise spicier and smokier.

Quick chipotle mayonnaise

If you are short of time, just add the chipotle to some ready-made mayonnaise and season with lime juice and a pinch of demerara sugar.

NOTE If you can't find chipotles, buy any smoked chilli sauce to use as your base instead.

100ml vegetable oil
1 tablespoon red wine vinegar
½ teaspoon caster sugar

Chipotle ketchup

There is nothing quite like home-made ketchup, particularly when matched with the earthy heat of chipotle. This is a lovely recipe to make with kids and eat with their fish fingers (go easy on the chipotles if they're not used to heat).

Heat the olive oil in a large pan and cook the onion over a medium-low heat until the onion starts turning translucent. Add the garlic and keep cooking until the onion starts taking the merest hint of colour.

Add the tomatoes and their juices to the pan, crushing the tomatoes with the back of a spoon. Stir in the rest of the ingredients, bring to the boil and then simmer for an hour, stirring occasionally.

After an hour, purée the mixture, and then continue to cook over a low heat until it reaches your desired thickness and looks like ketchup.

The ketchup can be stored in clean, sterilized bottles in the fridge for several months.

NOTE Home-made ketchup makes a popular present. You may want to double the recipe rather than find yourself left with none.

Makes approx. 1.5 litres

Cooking time:
1–1½ hours

2 tablespoons olive oil
1 very large Spanish onion or 2–3 medium-sized ones, halved and sliced
8 cloves of garlic, peeled and sliced
1.5kg ripe tomatoes (or tinned plum tomatoes),
1 stick of celery, chopped
125ml cider vinegar
70g demerara sugar
½ cinnamon stick
1 teaspoon celery salt
½ teaspoon mustard powder
½ teaspoon cloves
1 piece of mace
2 teaspoons coriander seeds
2 teaspoons black peppercorns
2 bay leaves
1–2 tablespoons Chipotles en adobo (see page 36)
sea salt

Tomato & Chilli
Jam

Pink
Pickled
Onions

STRAWBERRY JAM

CHIPOTLE KETCHU

An easy-peasy peanut mole

Makes enough for 4

Cooking time:
1 hour (or 30 minutes if you
cook the sauce without the
chicken)

1 onion, cut into quarters
3 cloves of garlic
2 medium tomatoes
180g unsalted peanuts
110g sesame seeds
1 teaspoon sea salt
5 cloves, ground
4 allspice berries
½ stick cinnamon
1 teaspoon tamarind puree
1 tablespoon cider vinegar
1 teaspoon sugar
2 tablespoon Chipotles en
    adobo (see page 36)
30g lard or vegetable oil
12 chicken thighs
500ml water
chopped flat-leaf parsley,
    to garnish

**Flavoured with smoky chipotles and tangy tamarind,
this recipe couldn't be simpler, nor the taste more addictive.**

Preheat the oven to the highest setting. Put the onion, garlic
and tomato in a roasting pan and roast the garlic for about
8 minutes until soft and the onion and tomato for about
15 minutes until blackened and soft.

Meanwhile toast the peanuts in a dry frying pan until golden
then grind to a powder. Repeat with the sesame seeds, being
careful not to burn. Mix the two together with a teaspoon of
sea salt (you can grind it with the nuts). Reserve a few
tablespoons of this for sprinkling on the mole at the end.

Grind the spices and add them to a blender with the rest of
the seasonings, the Chipotles, tomatoes, onion and garlic.
Add the ground nuts and seeds and about 100ml water, just
enough to loosen the blades and whizz up to a smooth purée.

Heat a pan until smoking hot and add the fat, followed by
the chicken thighs, skin side down. Sauté for about 5
minutes, until the skin is crispy and golden before turning
and sautéing on the other side for a few minutes. Remove
the chicken and add the sauce to the pan, stirring constantly
to avoid burning the mole. Cook for a few minutes and then
turn the heat down and continue to stir for another few
minutes. Add the rest of the water and the chicken and
cook over a gentle heat for about 25 minutes, or until the
chicken is cooked. Garnish with some chopped flat leaf
parsley and sprinkle with the reserved ground nuts.

Mole Poblano

This recipe is slightly more complex but well worth the effort for its rich, chocolate-tinged deliciousness. It vastly improves after a day or two, so make in advance.

Roast the onion, garlic and tomatoes in the oven for 20 minutes, or until blackened in parts. Cover the chillies with boiling water and simmer for 15 minutes until they are completely soft.

Meanwhile, heat a heavy-bottomed frying pan over a medium heat and add a tablespoon of lard. When it is sizzling, add the almonds and fry until they are a pale gold all over. Remove with a slotted spoon and add the walnuts, stirring as you fry them. Remove and add to the almonds. Add more fat and fry the prunes for a few minutes, until they start to caramelize, and then add to the nuts. Repeat with the raisins until they are puffed up and golden, and then the plantain, frying until golden. Fry the brioche bread and add to the fried ingredients.

Lastly, fry the sesame seeds until they are golden. Fry the rest of the spices for a few minutes just to release the aromatics. With a pestle and mortar or spice grinder, grind the sesame seeds, spices and oregano to a paste and add to the rest of the fried ingredients. Drain the chillies and add them to a blender with the Chipotles, pouring in just enough stock to release the blades and enable you to whiz the chillies to a smooth purée. Add the fried ingredients with another cup of stock so that you have a thick, smooth paste, adding more stock if you are putting too much pressure on your machine.

Heat 50g of lard in a casserole pan and when it is sizzling hot, pour in the puréed sauce and cook, stirring constantly, for about 5 minutes over a medium heat, being very careful not to burn the sauce. Add the rest of the stock and a cup of water, season with plenty of salt and pepper and the sugar and cook over a low heat for about 20 minutes, allowing the flavours to blend. Stir in the chocolate and simmer for another 10 minutes or until you start seeing fat rise to the surface. This is the sign that the mole is cooked.

Cooking time:
1½ hours

1 onion, cut into quarters
8 cloves of garlic, skin left on
2 tomatoes
80g mulatto chillies,
    destalked and deseeded
40g pasilla chillies,
    destalked and deseeded
30g ancho chillies,
    destalked and deseeded
125g lard
80g almonds
60g walnuts
80g prunes, roughly chopped
60g raisins
1 plantain, sliced up
½ brioche bun, torn up
    into small pieces
90g sesame seeds
3 allspice berries
4 cloves
2 petals from a star anise
½ cinnamon stick
a good pinch of dried
    oregano
1 tablespoon Chipotles
    en adobo (see page 36)
1.5 litres chicken stock
    (fresh or from a cube)
sea salt and black pepper
3 tablespoons demerara
    or cane sugar
100g dark chocolate (70%
    cocoa solids), chopped

CHAPTER 2

Nibbles
& side dishes

From Pickled jalapeños to Spicy nuts, these nibbles are the perfect thing to stave off hunger pangs and delight guests

I am always happy to see Guacamole in any guise, whether it is a simple avocado, salt and lime mash, where you can really taste the delicate flavour of the avocado, or a pestle and mortar job with garlic, coriander and diced chillies. Place alongside a plate of Pork scratchings, home-made or otherwise, and if you are into piggy bits, it is a match made in heaven.

Of course, as well as learning about things to nibble, it is also vital to know how to cook Mexico's two essential side dishes: the **perfect rice** and the **best-ever refried beans**.

These recipes would be nothing without the herbs listed below. Most of these will be familiar to you, but used in the right way they can add a distinctly Mexican flavour to your cooking.

Mint Usually added to recipes towards the end of cooking. Many different varieties are grown in Mexico and they go well with corn, tomatoes, courgettes and beans.

Thyme Used in Mexico as an aromatic to flavour soups, stocks and stews.

Coriander The most widely used herb in the world, and also in Mexican cooking. Add at the last minute to fresh salsas, as a garnish for soups and stews, or serve roughly chopped alongside bowls of finely chopped onion and wedges of lime to dress up tacos, tortillas, etc.

Oregano Used fresh and dried throughout Mexico. If you do use the dried stuff, make sure it hasn't been lurking in your cupboard for too long or it may taste musty.

Tarragon and **Chervil** Both have the subtle flavour of anise that is found in less readily available Mexican herbs. I use them together with the flavour of a fresh bay leaf when I am looking for a distinctly Mexican flavour.

Bay leaves Used fresh to add flavour to soups, stews and other dishes.

Mint

Thyme

Coriander

Oregano

Tarragon

Bay leaves

Chervil

A classic guacamole

Makes enough for 6

Preparation time:
20 minutes

½ red onion, very finely
  chopped
1–2 serrano or other fresh
  green chillies, finely
  chopped
1–2 teaspoons sea salt
3 ripe Hass avocados
juice of 1–2 limes
a small handful of coriander
  leaves, chopped
black pepper

Guacamole can be translated from the Aztec as 'avocado' (guac) 'sauce' (mole). The secret to a good one is to use ripe avocados, masses of fresh coriander and really mash up the chilli to a paste before you even think about adding the rest of the ingredients.

Put a quarter of the onion and half the chilli and salt in a pestle and mortar and mash to a rough paste.

Cut open the avocados, remove the stones and scoop out the flesh into the mortar (or into a large bowl if your mortar is small).

Roughly mash the flesh with a fork, adding half the lime juice as you go. When you have a rough guacamole, stir in the rest of the lime juice, red onion and chilli and the coriander.

Season with plenty of black pepper and more salt if you think it needs it. If it doesn't taste delicious by this stage, think whether it might need more lime juice or coriander.

Serve the guacamole with freshly made Totopos (tortilla chips) (see page 113) or bought tortilla chips.

Guacamole with tomato and garlic
Add 1 small clove of garlic in the first step and mash up with the chilli and onion, then add 1 very ripe deseeded and diced tomato at the end.

A winter guacamole
Add the seeds from half a pomegranate to your classic guacamole. The colours are wonderful.

Pork scratchings

Makes a large bowl
of scratchings

Cooking time:
up to 2 hours +
4 hours drying time

a large piece of pork skin
  from your butcher
  (weighing about 600g)

For the seasoning salt
1 heaped teaspoon
  black peppercorns
1 teaspoon allspice berries
1 teaspoon fennel seeds
1 tablespoon finely chopped
  sage leaves
zest of an orange
2 heaped tablespoons
  sea salt

Chicharrón, aka pork scratchings, are the national snack
in Mexico, served with guacamole and an ice-cold beer.
This recipe is exceedingly cheap to make as most butchers
will give you pork skin for nothing. It takes a little seasoning
time, but is definitely worth the effort.

Grind the pepper, allspice and fennel in a pestle and mortar
or spice grinder and mix with the sage, orange zest and salt.

Cut the pork skin into pieces roughly half the size of a credit
card. Depending how fatty you like your scratchings, you can
trim off some of the fat. Bring a saucepan of water to the boil,
drop in the rinds and simmer for 10 minutes. Drain the pieces,
pat them dry and allow to cool. Rub the spiced salt into the pork
skin well and leave out on a rack, either in the fridge or over old
newspaper in the airing cupboard for at least 4 hours, until the
skin is dry.

Preheat the oven to its highest setting and place the rinds
in a single layer on two baking trays. Put the rinds in the
oven and roast the skin for about 10 minutes (be careful
not to burn them), then immediately turn the oven down to
170°C/325°F/gas 3.

Roast the rinds for about 30 minutes until crisp but not too
blackened, draining off the fat every so often into a ceramic
dish. You can keep this fat in the fridge for cooking with and
add to it every time you cook bacon.

When they are done, the rinds should be puffed up and
golden, but not burnt. When they are looking good enough
to eat, you should do so at once with plenty of guacamole
(see page 48) and a glass of fine ale or tequila.

Mini avocado tostadas

Small tortilla circles are fried until crisp and topped with an assortment of fresh ingredients or salads. The purée is bright green, whilst the two different toppings, vegetarian and non, give you a kaleidoscope of sparkly reds, greens and pinks.

Preheat the oven to 200°C/400°F/gas 6. First off, brush the corn tortilla rounds on both sides with the oil and bake until golden and crisp, about 5 minutes.

For the avocado purée, heat the olive oil in a small frying-pan. Sweat the shallots for 5 to 10 minutes until turning translucent, and then add the garlic and chillies. Season well with salt and pepper and cook for another few minutes. Add the avocado flesh and half the lime juice and cook for another 5 minutes, mashing up the flesh with the back of a wooden spoon. Transfer to a bowl, whiz to a smooth purée with a stick blender and check for seasoning, adding more salt, pepper and lime if you think it needs it.

Meanwhile, slice the ham into random pieces, small enough to fit astride the tortilla rounds. Place on a baking sheet and bake in the oven for about 5 minutes until crisp (be careful, they are incredibly easy to burn).

To assemble, spread a layer of the avocado purée on the tostadas and spoon a little pile of the salsa on half of them. On the other half, top with a slice of the crisp ham. Pop onto platters and put on the table. Serve with chopped coriander.

Mini avocado tortillas or crostini

If you can't get hold of corn tortillas, use flour tortillas. Alternatively, make crostini by slicing skinny baguettes into thin slices, brushing them with oil and baking them in an oven at 180°C/350°F/gas 4 until golden.

Feeds 6–10 for a starter or nibbles

Preparation time:
30 minutes

a packet of corn tortillas,
   cut into bite size circles
   (use a pastry cutter or cut
   round a glass)
vegetable or olive oil
10–12 slices of Parma ham
1 x Fresh tomato salsa
   (see page 26)

For the avocado purée
4 tablespoons olive oil
5 shallots, finely chopped
2 cloves of garlic, crushed
1 chile de arbol or
   2 small dried red chillies
sea salt and black pepper
the flesh of 5–6 large
   Hass avocados
juice of 1–2 limes
a large handful of coriander
   leaves, roughly chopped

Spicy nuts

Makes 2 cups

Cooking time:
1 hour

2 teaspoons cumin seeds
1–2 tablespoons dried
   chilli flakes
500g raw peanuts, in their
   skins
2 tablespoons vegetable oil
1 head of garlic, broken up
   but with skin still on
5–6 sprigs of thyme leaves
juice of 2 limes
2 tablespoons extra fine
   sea salt

These hot, zingy nuts can be found in cantinas all over Mexico and are utterly moreish.

Preheat the oven to 150°C/300°F/gas 2. Gently warm the cumin seeds in a dry frying pan, then grind them together with the chilli in a pestle and mortar or spice grinder.

Toss the peanuts in the oil and roast for 30 minutes before adding the garlic cloves, thyme leaves and spice mix. Roast for a further 30 minutes, stirring from time to time. By this time the peanuts should be crunchy and toasted, but sometimes they need a little longer, so don't be afraid to cook them for up to 30 minutes more.

The second you have taken the nuts out of the oven, sprinkle them with the lime juice and most of the salt. Leave them spread out to cool (if you store them immediately they will go soggy). Check the seasoning after about 10 minutes and add the rest of the salt if you think they need it.

Smoky, grilled corn cob

Corn on the cob is sold all over Mexico. I find the smoky flavour of Chipotle with the sweetness of corn dripping in butter a pretty stunning combination.

Preheat the grill to its highest setting or heat a griddle pan or barbecue. Peel back the corn husks without actually tearing them off, remove any of the strands of silk and then cover again in the husks. Run briefly under a tap to prevent them burning on the heat and grill for 7 to 8 minutes, turning them at intervals so that they are grilled all over.

Meanwhile, melt the butter in a pan and smash the garlic clove with the heel of your hand or a rolling pin. Peel off the skin and add to the butter. When the butter is melted, add the Chipotles and stir until they have melted into the butter. Remove the garlic and season the sauce well with salt, pepper and the lime juice. Pour over the corn.

Serve with wedges of the remaining half lime and, if you like, scattered with fresh coriander. If you couldn't find Chipotles, sprinkle with the cayenne pepper at the end.

Mexican street corn
Serve the grilled corn drizzled with mayonnaise or sour cream, cayenne pepper, fresh lime and a scattering of grated Pecorino or Lancashire cheese. If you want to be healthy, just lime juice, salt and cayenne pepper is delicious.

NOTE If you have bought naked corn out of the husk, simmer in salted, boiling water for 4 to 5 minutes before grilling as above.

Cooking time:
30 minutes

4 corn on the cobs,
    in their husks
75g butter
1 clove of garlic
1 tablespoon Chipotles en
    adobo, finely chopped
    (optional) (see page 36)
    or a light sprinkling of
    cayenne pepper
sea salt and black pepper
juice of ½ lime

Cheese & chilli bites

Feeds 6–10 for a starter
or nibbles

Preparation time:
30 minutes

at least a litre of
   vegetable oil
a packet of corn tortillas,
   cut into bite-size pieces
2–3 serrano chillies (or
   any fresh green chillies)
150g hard goat's or sheep's
   cheese (like Ticklemore
   or Berkswell)
150g quince jam

These little bites can be served as nibbles before eating or as small starters. Crisp corn, sweet goat's cheese and quince jam show off the flavour of the green chilli beautifully.

Heat the oil until shimmering hot. If the oil bubbles up vigorously, then it is up to temperature. If the oil doesn't move very much, wait for the temperature to rise further.

Fry the corn discs in batches until they are golden and crisp. Fish them out with a slotted spoon and drain on kitchen paper.

Alternatively, preheat the oven to 200°C/400°F/gas 6, brush the corn tortilla rounds on both sides with oil and bake until golden and crisp, about 5 minutes.

Slice the chillies into wafer-thin rounds. Put a small slice of goat's cheese on each disc and smear with a little of the quince jam. Top with a slice of green chilli and serve before dinner (maybe with some guacamole and chips).

Mexican crudités

This is a light dish for when the weather is hot and you need something to quench your thirst. I love to arrange it on plates and hand round with drinks, but it is also a great way to start the day and makes a lovely pudding – the cucumber, fresh mango and pineapple dusted in chilli-lime salt.

Cut the pineapple lengthways down the middle, and then each half into half again to get long wedges. Cut out the inner core of each wedge and chop the flesh into cubes. Cut the cucumber into similar-shaped chunks. Peel the mango and cut the flesh into long stick shapes.

Grind all the chilli salt ingredients in a spice grinder or in a pestle and mortar.

Serve the fruit and vegetables arranged fetchingly on plates with little pots of the salt to dip into.

NOTE If you can't get mangoes, use whatever fruit is in season, such as apples, plums and peaches.

Serves 4

Preparation time:
20 minutes

1 small pineapple, peeled
1 cucumber, peeled and
   seeds removed
1–2 mangoes

For the chilli salt
2 tablespoons sea salt
4 chiles de arbol or
   8 small dried red chillies
zest of 3 limes
2 tablespoons caster sugar
½ teaspoon cumin seeds

Prawn coctel

Coctels are eaten up and down the coastlines of Mexico. Mexicans seem to have almost as big a passion for Tabasco and Worcestershire sauce as we do. Think of this starter as half prawn cocktail, half Bloody Mary. It balances sweet, juicy prawns with a fiery, sweet tomato juice marinade – I love it!

For the marinade
500ml tomato juice
2 heaped tablespoons
    ketchup
juice of 2 oranges,
    freshly squeezed
juice of 3 limes
1–2 tablespoon grenadine
3 tablespoons
    Worcestershire sauce
1 tablespoon of Tabasco
sea salt and black pepper
2 tablespoons Tequila

For the salad
300g cooked shrimp
300g fresh scallops, diced
½ cucumber
3 spring onions, finely
    chopped
8 cherry tomatoes, quartered
½ avocado, diced
½ habanero chilli, deseeded
    and finely diced (optional)
1 baby gem shredded
A small handful of coriander
    leaves, chopped

Mix the tomato juice, ketchup, orange juice, lime juice, grenadine, Worcestershire sauce, Tabasco, tequila, salt and pepper together in a jug and check for seasoning. You are looking for a nice balance of fire to pep you up, saltiness to season the whole cocktail, refreshing citrus kick from the orange and lime and sweetness to balance the rest of the flavours. Stir in the scallops and chill this liquid in the fridge for at least an hour so the citrus can start cooking the scallops.

Cut the cucumber in half lengthways and scoop out the seeds with a small spoon. Finely dice the flesh into 4–5mm cubes and do the same with the avocado. Stir in the prawns, tomatoes, coriander and spring onions.

Put a small layer of shredded lettuce in the bottom of six glasses and spoon over the coctel with all it juices. Serve with salty crackers, as they do in Mexico, or buttered, brown bread.

Pickled vegetables

Preparation time:
1 hour

10–12 jalapeño chillies
100ml olive oil
2 large red onions, halved
   and sliced into
   5mm semicircles
½ head of cauliflower,
   broken up
2 large carrots, sliced on
   the bias
12 cloves of garlic, peeled
   and sliced lengthways
   in half
1 bunch of radishes, topped
   and cut in half
1 teaspoon coriander seeds
½ teaspoon peppercorns
6 allspice berries, battered
   with a rolling pin
3 bay leaves
4 sprigs of thyme
a good pinch of dried oregano
2 tablespoons brown sugar
2 tablespoons sea salt
1 teaspoon Dijon mustard
500ml good-quality
   cider vinegar
50ml sherry

These are an ideal light tapas to pick at with a drink before your meal and they spice up tacos and quesadillas beautifully. They strike me as very British (think piccalilli and pickled onions) despite being quintessentially Mexican.

Slice the chillies on the bias, trying to keep as many of the seeds as possible – they will release their heat into the pickle. Heat the oil in a large pan and add the onion, cauliflower, carrot, garlic and chilli. Sauté over a medium heat for 5 to 10 minutes until the vegetables start to soften, but still have a bit of BITE! Add the rest of the ingredients and 250ml water and bring to the boil. Simmer for a minute or two and then turn off the heat.

Check the seasoning, adding more sugar, salt or vinegar to balance the flavours. Allow the vegetables to cool in the pickle.

Packed in sterilized glass jars and refrigerated, they will last for at least a month. Try not to touch for 3 days as the vegetables mellow in their pickle and become increasingly delicious!

Aguachile

Makes 6

This is a really delicious little starter: bites of fresh fish suspended in a blend of lime juice, fish sauce and fiery hot chillies. The translation of Aguachile from Spanish is 'chilli water' and served in beautiful Moroccan tea glasses, it is like drinking a shot of the sea laced with fire. Serve just enough to whet the appetite.

Juice the limes and then blend the juice in a blender with the chillies, spring onion, garlic, palm sugar and fish sauce. Season to taste.

Peel the cucumber, cut into quarters, lengthways, and spoon out the seeds. Cut crosswise into dice.

Divide the scallops and cucumber among six small glasses and top with the aguachile. Refrigerate until you are ready to eat and serve sprinkled with a little fresh coriander and the tortilla chips.

Preparation time:
20 minutes

250ml lime juice (6–8 limes)
5 serrano chillies or
    other hot, fresh green
    chillies, deseeded
2 spring onions, chopped
1 clove of garlic, chopped
5 teaspoons palm sugar
1 tablespoon fish sauce
1 teaspoon sea salt
8–10 scallops (about 180g),
    finely diced
½ cucumber

To serve
a small handful of coriander
    leaves, chopped
tortilla chips

✳ ✳ ✳ ✳ ✳ ✳ ✳

Preparation time:
20 minutes

2–3 plum tomatoes
225g sea bass, skinned
  and diced into 1cm cubes
juice of 5–6 limes
4 tablespoons coconut milk
1 tablespoon olive oil
a pinch of sea salt
½ small red onion,
  finely diced
1 clove of garlic, finely
  chopped
1 habanero (Scotch bonnet)
  chilli, finely diced
a large handful of coriander
  leaves, chopped

To serve
chopped coriander leaves
4–5 radishes, finely sliced
½ avocado, peeled, stoned,
  roughly diced and tossed
  in the juice of ½ lime
Totopos (tortilla chips)
  (see page 113)

Coconut ceviche

In ceviche, the lime juice 'cooks' the raw fish, resulting in a beautifully light, delicious starter that requires very little work.

Cover the tomatoes with boiling water and count to 20. Drain and pierce them with a knife so that the skins slip off easily. Deseed and dice the tomatoes into 1cm cubes.

Place the fish in a glass bowl, add the lime juice, coconut milk, olive oil, salt, onion, garlic and chilli. Cover and refrigerate for at least an hour for a light marinade or 4 hours in total if you want the fish to be completely 'cooked'. The flesh of the bass will turn from translucent to opaque and white when it is completely cooked.

Drain the fish of the marinade, keeping it aside. Add the tomato and coriander to the fish and gently mix together, adding some of the marinade back into the fish if it looks dry.

Spoon the ceviche onto small starter plates and sprinkle over the chopped coriander, sliced radishes and diced avocado. Hand out tortilla chips to scoop up and eat the ceviche.

Summer mango ceviche
Omit the tomatoes and dice up the flesh of 2 small mangoes when they are in season in the summer.

Winter pomegranate ceviche
Omit the tomatoes and add the seeds of 2 pomegranates for a delicious winter ceviche.

As a main course
Just up the quantities and increase the amount of chilli. Serve with grilled, buttered sweet corn and roasted sweet potato, both of which calm the fiery nature of the ceviche.

Cooking black beans

Makes 600g cooked black beans

Cooking time:
2–3 hours

250g dried black beans
4 cloves of garlic, bashed
   with a rolling pin
a few sprigs of thyme
a few bay leaves
fresh epazote or ¼ teaspoon
   anise seeds (optional)
1 onion, cut in quarters
1 tablespoon sea salt

Beans are the mainstay of Mexican food and black beans are one of the most popular types, used to make the irresistible Frijoles refritos (see opposite).

Rinse the beans well in cold water and drain, picking out any loose pebbles. If you have the time, you can soak the beans overnight, which will reduce the overall cooking time. Place the beans in a large pan and cover with at least 10cm of cold water.

Add the garlic, herbs and onion and bring the water to the boil. Cook the beans until they are just soft, topping them up with boiling water if the water looks like it is boiling off and skimming off any white foam that gathers on the surface. This can take anything from 2 to 3 hours, depending on whether you soaked them overnight or not. At this stage, season the beans with the salt and continue to cook for another 15 to 20 minutes so that the beans absorb the flavour. If you add the salt any sooner, it prevents the beans from softening.

Drain the beans and remove the herbs, onion and garlic.

NOTE This recipe can also be used to cook dried chickpeas, borlotti, pinto, flor de mayo or any other beans you can find.

Frijoles refritos (refried beans)

In Mexico, refried beans are served with everything. Refrito means 'well-fried' and this is key. Cook them slowly in plenty of fat and you will taste their magic. Not necessarily a great recipe if you are on a diet. (I hate diets!)

Whiz the beans with a stick blender, adding just enough of the reserved cooking liquid to get a smooth, fairly thick purée.

Heat the fat in a heavy-bottomed pan (the heavy base will disperse the heat better, stopping the beans from catching quite so easily) and when it is gently foaming, add the onion. Season well with salt and pepper and sweat the onion until it is soft. Add the garlic, chilli (if you want a touch of spice) and herbs, cooking for a further few minutes.

Add the puréed beans to the onion mixture and cook for another 10 minutes, turning down the heat after a few minutes to very low and stirring constantly. Add a little more of the cooking liquid so that you get a nice smooth purée that falls easily from a wooden spoon. Taste and season again. At this stage, you can cool the beans and reheat them when you are ready to eat (cover them with a circle of greaseproof paper or old butter papers to stop the beans forming a skin).

When you are ready to eat, drizzle with the sour cream and scatter over the crumbled cheese and fresh coriander leaves. Serve with a bowl of Totopos (see page 113) or bought tortilla chips.

Chorizo refried beans
Top the beans with sautéed chorizo, onion and fresh coriander

WHY NOT TRY Refried beans are delicious drizzled with habanero salsa (see page 30) or served with steak and chipotle butter (see page 38)

Cooking time:
30 minutes

600g cooked black beans
  (see opposite page), with the
  cooking liquid reserved
at least 50g lard, butter or
  olive oil
1 white onion, finely chopped
sea salt and black pepper
2 cloves of garlic,
  finely chopped
½ chile de arbol,
  finely chopped (optional)
1 tablespoon chopped
  coriander root or stalks
  or epazote
a few fresh bay leaves

To finish
a knob of butter
sour cream
50g Lancashire or Cheshire
  cheese, crumbled
freshly chopped
  coriander leaves

Red rice

Serves 4

Cooking time:
45 minutes

220g basmati rice
400g tin plum tomatoes
1 tablespoon tomato purée
2 tablespoons olive
  or vegetable oil
1 onion, finely chopped
1 jalapeño chilli,
  finely chopped
1 clove of garlic, crushed or
  finely chopped
sea salt and black pepper
500ml chicken stock (fresh or
  from a cube)
50g carrot, diced
50g frozen peas

Put the rice in a sieve and rinse in cold water until the water runs clear. This will stop the rice sticking together later.

Heat the oil in a heavy-bottomed saucepan and add the onion, sautéing for a few minutes before adding the chilli and garlic. Continue cooking until the onion has turned translucent before adding the rice, tomatoes and purée. Cook for about 5 minutes, breaking up the tomatoes with a wooden spoon, and season with salt and pepper.

Add the stock and continue to simmer. After another 5 minutes, add the carrot and peas and cook for about 10 minutes or until the liquid has been absorbed and the rice is cooked. Taste, checking for seasoning.

Remove from the heat, cover well with butter papers or greaseproof paper and a lid and let the rice stand in a low oven (120°C/225°F/gas 1) for at least 10 minutes or for up to 2 hours.

Green rice

Serves 4

Cooking time:
30 minutes

400g basmati rice
1 small clove of garlic
1 small onion
2 large handfuls of coriander
a large bunch of parsley
  or spinach
4 tablespoons olive oil
600ml chicken or vegetable
  stock (fresh or from a cube)
  or water
sea salt and black pepper

The delicate flavour of this rice goes beautifully with fish or chicken, whilst its wonderful emerald green colour makes a pretty addition to any table of food.

Rinse the rice under cold water until the water runs clear.

Whiz the garlic, onion and greens in a food processor with a splash of water and half the olive oil until you have a thick green purée. Heat the remaining oil in a saucepan and when hot, add the purée and fry for 5 minutes, stirring so as not to burn.

Add the rice and stir well to combine. Pour in the stock and simmer for about 15 minutes until most of the liquid has been absorbed. Cover with butter papers or greaseproof paper and a lid and put in a low oven (120°C/225°F/gas 1) for 30 minutes to finish cooking. Taste, checking for seasoning.

CHAPTER 3

Soups

I could fill an entire book with the soups of Mexico.

Despite it being such a hot country, they are on every menu, using ingredients in season and flavoured with herbs, spices and chillies. This chapter has eight easy and unusual soup recipes that are simple to put together, but full of intriguing flavours.

With every part of an animal used in Mexican recipes, bones and vegetable off-cuts are employed to make aromatic stocks, while poaching or braising meat also produces stock as a by-product. Recipes like Sopa de lima and Herby mushroom soup are all about the stock, while others like the the Minty courgette soup are all about the main ingredient.

I love these soups at any time of day, as a starter or as a main meal.

Chilled avocado soup

Serves 4

Cooking time:
25 minutes

3 large ripe Hass avocados,
    peeled and stoned
1 tablespoon chopped chives
1 tablespoon chopped
    coriander leaves
juice of 1 lime
1 small clove of garlic
1½ pints chicken stock
    (fresh or from a cube), chilled
½ teaspoon grated nutmeg
sea salt and black pepper

Deep-fried ancho chillies
vegetable or sunflower oil,
    for frying
2 ancho chillies

To serve
crème fraîche
1 tablespoon finely chopped
    chives

I like to serve this soup in small bowls because it is so rich and I tend only to make it when I have a good stock. I use creamy Hass avocados and serve the soup with either Totopos (tortilla chips – see page 113) or these deep-fried ancho chillies, which are also delicious in salads or on refried beans.

Purée the avocados, herbs, lime juice, garlic and a third of the chicken stock in a food processor or preferably a blender (to get a smoother finish). Pour the mixture into a large bowl. Add the remaining stock, nutmeg and plenty of salt and pepper. Season to taste, adding more seasoning if you think it needs it. It will take quite a bit of salt. Cover and chill.

Heat enough oil in a small saucepan so that it is thumb deep. Meanwhile, tear out the stems of the ancho chillies and all the seeds. Tear the chillies up into small pieces. When the oil is shimmering hot, throw in the ancho pieces and fry for a few seconds until they puff up and turn light and crispy (test one by biting into it, trying not to burn your tongue!). Immediately fish the pieces out with a slotted spoon as they burn very easily.

Serve the soup in individual bowls with a little teaspoon of crème fraîche, the chives and the deep-fried chilli pieces.

Minty courgette soup

There must be at least a hundred versions of courgette soup in Mexico, with corn, chillies, tomatoes, different herbs. This is an incredibly simple one, allowing the courgettes to be the centre of attention. It makes an elegant starter or light lunch.

Gently warm the olive oil in a wide saucepan and add the garlic and chilli. Cook for a minute or two without colouring before adding the courgettes. Season well with salt and pepper.

Cook the courgettes over a medium-low heat for 30 minutes, adding 300ml water after 20 minutes when the courgettes should have released some of their own water and will be soft and mushy. Cook for a little longer if they are not all quite soft.

Check for seasoning and blitz for about 15 to 20 seconds with a stick blender. You want a lovely thick soup with a rough consistency, not a smooth soup.

Serve the soup in warmed bowls, sprinkled with the mint and Pecorino and drizzled with a little more extra virgin olive oil.

WHY NOT TRY This makes a stunning lunch served with the Cheese & courgette filo parcels on page 132.

Serves 6

Cooking time:
35 minutes

3 tablespoons extra virgin
   olive oil, plus extra for
   drizzling
4 cloves of garlic, chopped
1 chile de arbol or 2 small
   dried red chillies,
   finely chopped
1kg courgettes,
   roughly sliced
sea salt and black pepper
a small handful of mint
   leaves, roughly chopped
grated Pecorino cheese

Corn & green chilli soup

Serves 6

Cooking time:
1 hour

2 tablespoons olive oil
a knob of butter
2 white onions, sliced
3 cloves of garlic, chopped
3 sticks of celery, chopped
1 head of fennel, chopped
1 green poblano chilli,
   deseeded and chopped
3–4 coriander roots and
   stalks, washed and
   chopped
7 heads of fresh corn, kernels
   removed from the cobs
about 1 litre vegetable
   stock (fresh or from a cube)
   or water
1 shallot, finely chopped
juice of 1 lime
sea salt and black pepper

To serve
about 100ml sour cream
2 tablespoons chopped
   coriander leaves

This is a lovely fresh-tasting soup to eat in the summer (or use frozen corn in other seasons).

In a heavy-bottomed pan, heat the olive oil and butter until gently foaming and then add the onions, garlic, celery, fennel, poblano chilli, coriander roots and stalks and two-thirds of the corn. Stir and cook over a medium heat for about 10 minutes until the vegetables start to soften.

When the onion has turned translucent, add enough vegetable stock or water to barely cover the vegetables and bring to the boil, simmering with the lid on for about 30 minutes until the vegetables are completely soft. Purée in a blender until smooth. If you want a silky smooth soup, push it through a sieve into a clean pan.

Meanwhile, sauté the shallot and remaining corn kernels in a frying pan over a high heat for a few minutes until the corn just starts taking some colour. Stir into the soup with the lime juice and season with salt and pepper. Cook for a few minutes more.

Pour the hot soup into six bowls, swirl in the sour cream and finish with a sprinkling of coriander. This soup is also delicious chilled.

NOTE If you can't get hold of a poblano chilli, use a green pepper instead and one or two fresh green chillies for a dusting of chilli heat.

Black bean sopa Azteca

There is something unfailingly comforting about black bean soup. It warms the soul and makes life feel good.

Heat a heavy-bottomed frying pan and dry roast the tomatoes and garlic (see method on page 28) for about 5 minutes until the garlic skin has blackened and charred in places. Remove the garlic and continue to roast the tomatoes for another 5 minutes until charred. Turn off the heat.

Meanwhile, heat the butter and olive oil in a large, heavy-bottomed pan and, when it is gently foaming, add the onion and herbs. Sweat for about 5 minutes until the onion is soft and then add the garlic, tomatoes and Chipotle purée, if you are using, seasoning well with salt and pepper. Cook for a few minutes before adding the beans and their cooking liquid. Cook for a few more minutes before adding the stock and lime juice and simmer gently for 10 to 15 minutes so that the flavours can develop.

Whiz briefly with a stick blender for a textured soup with a bit of bite or purée until smooth, depending on how you like your soup.

Slice the tortillas into thin strips and fry them gently in a pan with a little olive oil until golden and crisp. Drain on kitchen paper. You can also bake them in the oven if you prefer (see page 113).

Pour the soup into six bowls, sprinkle over the tortilla strips, scatter over the feta, the salsa, sour cream and the coriander leaf.

VARIATION Omit the Fresh tomato salsa and serve with the deep-fried ancho chillies (see page 68) for a more exotic flavour.

Serves 6

Cooking time:
35 minutes

2 plum tomatoes
3 cloves of garlic, skin on
25g butter or lard
1 tablespoon olive oil
½ white onion,
    finely chopped
1–2 tablespoons chopped
    oregano or marjoram or
    1 teaspoon dried oregano
2 fresh bay leaves
1–2 teaspoons Chipotle purée
    (optional) (see page 37)
sea salt and black pepper
600g cooked black beans
    (see page 62), with the
    cooking liquid reserved
500ml chicken or vegetable
    stock (fresh or from a cube)
juice of 1 lime

To serve
2 corn tortillas
olive oil
100g feta cheese, crumbled
100g Fresh tomato salsa
    (see page 26)
sour cream
a small handful of
    coriander leaves, chopped

Sweet & spicy squash & chickpea soup

Serves 2

This is an incredibly easy soup that you can whip up for a quick supper, but it is so delicious that I often give it to friends if they are coming over for dinner. It is rich and full of flavour with a lovely heat from the chilli oil.

Gently warm the cumin seeds in a dry frying pan, then grind them in a pestle and mortar or spice grinder.

For the chilli oil, mix the chillies and salt together in a small bowl and gradually add the olive oil. The oil should really only just cover the chilli, otherwise you are left with a lot of oil and not much chilli. Leave to infuse for 30 minutes before using.

Heat the olive oil in a large pan. Cook the leeks for 5 minutes over a medium heat until they are tender before adding the garlic, chilli, oregano and cumin. Cook for a further 3 minutes.

Add the squash, the cinnamon stick and bay leaf. Stir the squash into the leek mixture, then cover with the stock. Bring to the boil then turn the heat down and bring to a simmer. Cook for about 15 minutes or until the squash is soft but not falling apart. Add the chickpeas and season.

I like to either eat this soup as it is or just whiz it for a few seconds with a stick blender to get a lovely, rustic soup. However, you can liquidize it if you prefer a smooth soup.

Serve with the grated cheese sprinkled on top and drizzle each portion with some chilli oil.

Cooking time:
about 40 minutes

1 heaped teaspoon cumin seeds
2 tablespoons olive oil
2 small leeks, washed and roughly sliced
2 cloves of garlic, chopped
1 chile de arbol, finely chopped
5 sprigs of oregano or thyme, chopped
1 butternut squash (about 320g), peeled, deseeded and chopped into 2.5cm pieces
1 cinnamon stick
1 bay leaf
400ml chicken stock (fresh or from a cube)
220g cooked chickpeas (see page 84)
sea salt and black pepper
30g Lancashire cheese, grated

For the chilli oil (optional)
4 red chillies, cut in half lengthways, deseeded and finely diced (almost minced)
a generous pinch of sea salt
100ml extra virgin olive oil

Tortilla soup

Cooking time:
40 minutes

3 tablespoons lard or olive oil
2 onions, sliced
3 cloves of garlic, sliced
100g fine polenta
1 heaped tablespoon
   Chipotles en adobo
   (see page 36)
2 x 400g tins plum tomatoes
1 tablespoon brown sugar
1 teaspoon dried oregano
   or 1 tablespoon fresh
sea salt and black pepper
1.5 litres chicken or
   vegetable stock (fresh or
   from a cube)

For the garnishes
1 ripe Hass avocado
lemon or lime juice
300ml vegetable oil
   (which can be reused)
2 corn tortillas or 2 chapattis
2 ancho chillies, deseeded
   and stems removed
100g feta cheese, crumbled
a small handful of coriander
   leaves, chopped
100ml sour cream

Tortilla soup is as traditional to Mexico as French onion soup is to France. It never fails to delight newcomers with its beautiful presentation and deliciously complex flavours. If you cook just one thing from this book, cook this.

Heat the lard or oil in a large pan, add the onions and sweat over a medium heat for 10 to 15 minutes until the onion is completely soft before adding the garlic. Add the polenta and continue cooking for 5 minutes before adding the Chipotles, the tomatoes, sugar, oregano and seasoning. Cook for another 5 minutes, add the stock and simmer for a further 10 minutes. Blitz in a food processor until the soup is smooth. Leave over a low heat for at least 5 minutes before you eat.

Meanwhile, assemble all the garnishes for the soup. Halve the avocado, remove the stone, peel and dice the flesh, sprinkling with a little lemon or lime juice to stop it discolouring.

Heat the vegetable oil in a deep frying pan and cut the flat breads into thin, short 3cm strips. Tear up the ancho chillies into rough pieces. Test the oil and, when it is shimmering hot (and makes a tortilla strip sizzle), add the strips and cook until crisp and golden. Remove the pieces with a slotted spoon on to a plate lined with kitchen paper and fry the ancho chilli pieces until they have puffed up. This only takes a few seconds, so watch them like a hawk and try not to burn them or you will lose their lovely sweetness.

Serve the soup in bowls with all the garnishes laid out in small bowls or on plates so that people can help themselves at the table.

NOTE You can also add a rehydrated ancho chilli to the soup base for a rich, earthy flavour.

Sopa de lima

Feeds 4-6

Cooking time:
45 minutes

2 tomatoes
2–3 large chicken legs, on
    the bone
½ white onion
10 whole peppercorns
5 allspice berries
3 fresh bay leaves
3 tablespoons olive oil and a
    knob of butter
3 shallots, finely chopped
3 garlic cloves, roughly
    chopped
half a habanero (Scotch
    bonnet) chilli, deseeded and
    finely chopped
3 fresh bay leaves
a small handful fresh oregano
    leaves, chopped (or 3
    sprigs of thyme)
zest and juice from 3 limes
zest and juice of a pink
    grapefruit
at least a teaspoon of sea salt
pepper

To finish the soup
300ml vegetable oil (which
    can be reused)
2 corn tortillas or 2 chapattis
a large handful coriander
    leaves, roughly chopped
1 avocado, diced
½ white onion, finely chopped

Restorative and warming, this is the Mexican equivalent of a good, old-fashioned chicken soup – only more delicate and aromatic.

Pour boiling water over the tomatoes, wait 30 seconds and then peel them. Roughly chop the flesh.

Put the chicken legs, peppercorns, allspice and bay leaves into a pot and cover with 2 litres of water. Bring to the boil, turn the heat right down and simmer gently for 20 minutes. Remove the chicken and, when it is cool, shred the meat.

Warm the oil in a large saucepan over a medium heat and add the shallots. Cook gently for 5 minutes before adding the garlic, oregano and chilli. Sweat for a few minutes more before adding the tomatoes and zests, and seasoning with salt and pepper. After another 5 minutes, add the drained broth from the chicken, plus the bay leaves and the citrus juices. Simmer for 20 minutes over a low heat.

Heat the vegetable oil in a deep frying pan and cut the flat breads into thin, 3cm strips. Test the oil and, when it is shimmering hot (and makes a tortilla strip sizzle), add the strips and cook until crisp and golden. Remove the pieces with a slotted spoon onto a plate lined with kitchen paper.

Add the shredded chicken into the broth a few minutes before serving to heat through. Check the seasoning (it may need more salt). Serve the soup in hot bowls, scattered with the coriander, tortilla strips, avocado and chopped onion.

VARIATION: This is delicious with some finely shredded cabbage and carrot thrown in 5 minutes before the end.

Herby mushroom soup

This is a simple soup to make, the vegetables are dry roasted to get a real depth of flavour. There's a huge variety of mushroom in Mexico, just as there are over here, so try to mix a few wild ones in for a really authentic flavour.

Cut the stem off the chilli and place in a hot dry frying pan with the onion, garlic cloves and tomatoes. Dry roast the vegetables until their skins are starting to blacken (about 10 minutes for the garlic, onion and chilli and 15 minutes for the tomatoes), turning them from time to time so they are evenly cooked (see method on page 28). Peel the garlic cloves as they are cooked.

Meanwhile, in another (larger) frying pan, melt the butter or lard and when it is sizzling hot, add the mushrooms, seasoning them well with salt and pepper. Fry for at least 10 minutes over a medium-high heat until they have lost a lot of their juices and are beginning to take colour. Turn down the heat.

Whiz up the tomatoes, chilli, onion and garlic with the herbs and about a cup of the stock until you have a purée. Add this to the mushrooms along with the rest of the stock, seasoning well with more salt and pepper. Bring the soup to simmering point and let it gently simmer for 10 minutes so the flavours come together. Fry the rashers until they are crisp and cut up into small pieces.

Just before serving the soup, stir in the crème fraîche. Serve the soup at the table with the grated Pecorino, a scattering of coriander, another dollop of crème fraîche and the crisp fried bacon.

NOTE If you can get hold of some pasilla chillies, fry them as you would the anchos on page 68 and sprinkle them into the soup at the end instead of the bacon.

Cooking time:
40 minutes

1 jalapeño chilli
2 onions, cut into quarters
5 cloves of garlic, unpeeled
3 large, ripe tomatoes
a large knob of butter or lard
600g different types of
    mushrooms, sliced
sea salt and black pepper
1 leaf of hoja santa or
    ⅛ teaspoon ground anise
a handful of coriander leaves,
    roughly chopped
1 litre chicken or vegetable
    stock (fresh or from a cube)
150ml crème fraîche

To serve
6 rashers of thin streaky
    bacon (optional)
about 100g Pecorino cheese,
    freshly grated
chopped coriander leaves
extra creme fraîche

CHAPTER 4

Salads

Contrary to popular misconception, much of the food in Mexico is neither heavy nor greasy, but light and fiery and bursting with fresh flavour.

Simple shredded cabbage salads, fresh radishes, sliced onions and tomatoes are traditionally served as a balance to rich meat braises and chilli-spiked fish dishes. Nowadays more elaborate salads are being created in smart restaurants from Mexico City to Baja California, combining European and Mexican cooking techniques with local produce to create modern, delicious food. Chilli vinaigrettes, deep-fried chillies, fresh herbs like coriander, chervil and mint all play important roles in bringing these salads alive.

I've included a mix of classics (did you know that the Caesar salad was invented in Tijuana?) with a few more contemporary salads. Salads increasingly make up a popular part of the great Mexican long lunch, eaten as starters, like soups, before the many other courses that follow on these great, social occasions. They are also sometimes eaten as main courses or side dishes for shorter weekday lunches and are popular choices in the evenings when food is often much lighter than in the daytime.

The recipes in this chapter are a million miles away from Tex Mex sizzling fajitas and cheesy nachos.

A few easy and delicious salad dressings

Enough for a large salad

Preparation time:
5 minutes

1 clove of garlic
sea salt and black pepper
¼ habanero (Scotch bonnet)
    chilli, deseeded
juice of 1 large orange
juice of ½ lime
120ml extra virgin olive oil
a good pinch of achiote
    (optional)
a pinch of dried oregano

Caribbean chilli-citrus dressing

This dressing uses all the flavours of the Mexican Caribbean. The intense garlicky dressing packs a real punch and goes with the Citrusy chickpea salad on page 84 and the Fiery prawn and mango salad on page 93. Toss through flakes of just-cooked fish as a topping for tostadas.

Make the dressing by smashing the garlic, a pinch of salt and the chilli in a pestle and mortar. Mix in the citrus juices and olive oil, achiote, if using, and oregano and season with salt and pepper.

Enough for a salad for 6

Preparation time:
5 minutes

1 teaspoon cane or
    demerara sugar
1 teaspoon Dijon mustard
sea salt and black pepper
1 tablespoon balsamic
    vinegar
juice of ½ lime
6 tablespoons olive oil
1 tablespoon sesame oil

Sesame & balsamic dressing

Dressings like this one are hugely popular in Mexico City, where sushi is king and influences from Asian cooking crop up everywhere. As good on a simple avocado and watercress salad as on a more robust version like the Chicken and almond salad on page 86.

To make the dressing, mix the sugar, mustard, some salt and pepper, the vinegar and lime juice in a clean jam jar, a cup or a pestle and mortar. Mix until the sugar is dissolved and then stir in the oils. Check for seasoning, adding more salt, lime or sugar to adjust the balance of the flavours.

Chipotle vinaigrette

The smoky nature of Chipotles is toned down in this olive oil vinaigrette. The dressing goes with the Smoky asparagus salad on page 89, but also try it in avocado pears or just with a simple green salad.

Finely chop the chillies and mix with the rest of the dressing ingredients in a clean jam jar.

Enough for a large salad

Preparation time:
5 minutes

1–2 Chipotles en adobo
  (see page 36)
1 teaspoon Dijon mustard
1 teaspoon brown sugar
1 teaspoon balsamic
  vinegar
juice of ½ lime
200ml olive oil
sea salt and black pepper

Green chilli vinaigrette

This is a bright salad dressing that is perfect for green salads, but is also rather good with the Chicken and avocado salad on page 86.

Roast the chillies and garlic in a dry frying pan until they are blackened, blistered and soft. This will take about 5 to 10 minutes (see the method on page 28).

Remove the garlic skin and destem and deseed the chillies. Check the heat of the chillies with the tip of your tongue. If they are hot, you may only want to use one. Roughly chop them and put in a blender with the garlic, 3 tablespoons water and the rest of the ingredients (except the salt and pepper).

Blitz to a smoothish vinaigrette, season generously with salt and pepper, and serve at once (this dressing does not keep).

Preparation time:
15 minutes

2 green chillies
1 small clove of garlic
100ml extra virgin
  olive oil
2 tablespoons white wine
  vinegar
½ teaspoon caster sugar
a handful of coriander
  leaves, chopped
sea salt and black pepper

Citrusy chickpea salad

Preparation time:
25 minutes +
overnight soaking and
2 hours cooking for dried
chickpeas

300g dried chickpeas,
  soaked overnight
2 cloves of garlic
olive oil
5 small shallots,
  very finely sliced
a large handful of
  flat-leaf parsley
2 bay leaves
1 carrot, chopped
1 tablespoon sea salt
1 x Caribbean chilli-citrus
  dressing (see page 80)
a bunch of radishes,
  scrubbed and tops
  removed
2 sticks of celery

Chickpeas came to Mexico with the Arabs, who also brought spices and tamarind from Asia. I make this with the chilli-spiked dressing on page 80. It is lovely served just warm in the summer with some of the grilled recipes, particularly the barbecued monkfish (see page 161).

It is definitely worth cooking your own chickpeas for this recipe because it makes all the difference. Soak them overnight to make them softer and easier to cook the next day.

Smash the garlic cloves with the heel of your hand to break the skin and add them with a little olive oil to a pan together with a tablespoon of the shallots, a few sprigs of parsley, the bay leaves and carrot. Sweat for 5 minutes over a medium-high heat before adding the soaked chickpeas. Cover with cold water and bring to the boil, then simmer for about 2 hours until the chickpeas have swollen in size and are soft and tender. Add the salt after an hour of cooking.

Meanwhile, pour the dressing over the remaining sliced shallots and leave for 10 to 15 minutes to soften any acidic flavours.

Slice the radishes and celery very finely with a mandolin or sharp knife so that they are paper thin. Roughly chop the remaining parsley.

Drain the cooked chickpeas, discarding the bay, carrot and garlic. Toss the chickpeas in the dressing whilst still warm with the rest of the salad ingredients.

NOTE If you must use tinned chickpeas, drain, rinse and warm them up with a little olive oil in a pan before adding them to the dressing.

Fresh courgette & tomato salad

Feeds 6–8

This is a light salad that tastes of the summer. Use very ripe tomatoes and serve it with other dishes for a relaxed weekend lunch.

Put the shallot into a salad bowl with the vinegar, olive oil, sugar, salt and pepper and leave it to soften for 10 minutes.

Meanwhile, put the tomatoes in a large bowl and cover them with boiling water. Count to 20 and then drain. Skin them by piercing the tips of the tomatoes with a sharp knife and the skin will slip off easily. Quarter the tomatoes, scoop out the seeds and dice the flesh into small pieces. Add to the shallot.

Slice the courgettes into very fine rounds and toss with the shallot, tomatoes and mint. Serve immediately.

Courgette, feta & tomato salad
Turn this into a lunch dish by mixing in diced feta and some fried tortilla strips.

Preparation time:
10 minutes

1 shallot, finely chopped
2 tablespoons sherry vinegar
4 tablespoons olive oil
a pinch of sugar
sea salt and black pepper
500g very ripe tomatoes
2 courgettes
a large handful of mint
   leaves, finely chopped

A delicious chicken & avocado salad

Serves 6

Prepration time:
25 minutes

80g almonds
50g sesame seeds
1 small free-range chicken,
    poached (see page 140)
2 bunches of watercress
    or 1 large bag of
    watercress leaves
2 baby gems, separated
    into leaves
2 avocados, peeled, stoned
    and cut into chunks
2 shallots, finely sliced
1 x Sesame & balsamic
    dressing (page 80)
sea salt and black pepper

I love this salad. It is full of flavour, it is rich and satisfying and makes the perfect weekend lunch with fresh bread. The dressing uses Oriental influences that you find in many of the restaurants in Mexico City.

Toast the almonds in a dry frying pan until a pale golden. Remove and chop coarsely. Toast the sesame seeds in the same frying pan until golden and starting to pop out of the pan.

Tear the chicken into strips, mix with the watercress, baby gem, avocado chunks, shallots, almonds and sesame seeds and toss in the sesame dressing. Season with salt and pepper and serve.

NOTE If you are in a rush, use leftover cooked chicken and you can make the salad in 15 minutes.

A toasted almond & avocado salad
Leave out the chicken altogether and serve the green salad with grilled fish or after any main course. It is also yummy with the Green chilli vinagrette (page 83).

Mexico City's oriental ceviche

Serves 4

Preparation time:
20 minutes +
2 hours marinating

400g pollack, skinless
  and boneless, cut into
  2cm cubes
juice of 6–7 limes
juice of 1 pink grapefruit
a dash of good soy sauce
2 tablespoons best
  extra virgin olive oil
1 hot green chilli,
  finely diced
sea salt and black pepper
1 avocado
4 large handfuls of rocket
1 mango, peeled and
  chopped into 2cm cubes
4 spring onions, finely sliced
2 tablespoons coriander
  leaves, roughly chopped
a light sprinkling of
  toasted sesame seeds

This is an extremely simple salad using fish that has been 'cooked' in citrus juices and flavoured with soy sauce, an ingredient that travelled from the East to Mexico along with tamarind. It is worth using a decent extra virgin olive oil for the salad dressing – you'll really be able to taste the difference.

Place the fish in a glass bowl, add the lime and grapefruit juices, soy sauce, a tablespoon of the olive oil and the chilli. The fish should be totally covered with the marinade so that it all 'cooks' evenly in the citrus juices. Season with salt and pepper and leave to marinate for a few hours When you are ready to eat, pour off the marinade, reserving it for later.

Quarter and peel the avocado, discarding the stone, and slice each quarter into two or three slender slices. Lightly dress the rocket with a little of the marinade and a dash more of extra virgin olive oil and divide the rocket among four plates. Scatter the fish over the rocket salad with the mango, spring onions, slices of avocado and coriander. Drizzle with the remaining marinade, scatter with sesame seeds and serve with tortilla chips, brown bread and butter or salty crackers.

NOTE I use pollack in this recipe because there are still plenty left in the sea, but it is also delicious with fresh mackerel, line-caught sea bass, organic or wild salmon and rainbow trout.

Smoky asparagus

Serves 4–6

This is a delightful salad to eat in the late spring when asparagus is in season.

Steam the asparagus spears for 6 to 8 minutes or until *al dente*, tender but still with a little bite to them. Rinse them in cold water to stop them cooking any longer and cut in half.

Arrange all the salad ingredients in a bowl and toss with the dressing. Season to taste with salt and pepper.

Hand a slab of Parmesan around separately for people to grate over.

Preparation time:
20 minutes

2 bunches of asparagus,
   bases snapped off
2 avocados, peeled, stoned
   and diced
1 garden lettuce, torn
   into pieces
1 head of chicory, chopped
2 shallots, finely chopped
a handful of coriander leaves
1 x Chipotle vinaigrette
   (see page 81)
sea salt and black pepper
a slab of Parmesan cheese

The original Caesar salad

Preparation time:
30 minutes

For the salad
a head of cos lettuce
1 bag or 1 bunch of
    watercress
½ loaf of white country
    bread
100ml olive oil
the leaves of 4–5 sprigs of
    thyme
2 cloves of garlic, bashed
    with a rolling pin to release
    the flavour
sea salt and black pepper
a good few pinches of
    sweet pimentón
    (smoked paprika) (optional)
100g Pecorino or
    Parmesan cheese

For the dressing
2 egg yolks
juice of ½ lemon
a splash of red wine vinegar
a dash of Worcestershire
    sauce
1 teaspoon Dijon mustard
6 anchovy fillets (make sure
    they're sustainably caught),
    chopped
1 small clove of garlic, crushed
sea salt
100ml olive oil
100ml vegetable oil

The Caesar salad was created in Tijuana in 1924 by Caesar Cardini, an Italian restaurateur who apparently came up with the dish when a lunch rush depleted the kitchen's supplies. The classic combination of flavours is just delicious and it will always be a favourite of mine. This makes a glorious starter or light(ish) lunch.

Preheat the oven to 170°C/325°F/gas 3. To make the dressing, put the egg yolks, lemon juice, vinegar, Worcestershire sauce, mustard, anchovies and garlic into a food processor. Add a pinch of salt and blitz with the motor running. Gradually add the oils, beginning with a very slow, thin stream to get the mayonnaise started. Blend until you have a smooth mayonnaise, adding 1 to 2 tablespoons water towards the end to thin down the dressing.

Cut the lettuce in half lengthways and break up into the leaves. Wash all the salad leaves and dry.

Tear up the bread into rough, jagged chunks and toss in the olive oil, thyme, garlic, salt and pepper and a little paprika, if you like. Bake in the oven on a baking tray for 5 to 10 minutes until golden and crispy.

Season the cos and watercress leaves with salt and pepper and gently toss in the dressing with the croûtons. Grate the Pecorino cheese over the top of the salad with a potato peeler so you have lovely, big shavings of cheese.

Warm corn salad with a touch of spice

Feeds 4–6

Cooking time:
25 minutes

4 corn on the cobs
a slug of olive oil and
   a knob of butter
1 onion, finely chopped
1 green chilli,
   finely chopped
2 cloves of garlic, chopped
a few good pinches of
   allspice
sea salt and black pepper
juice of 1–2 limes
a handful of chopped
   coriander and mint leaves

To serve
sour cream
grated Pecorino or
   Parmesan cheese
a pinch of chilli powder
warm flat breads

This is an easy salad. The sweetness of the corn and the freshness of the herbs are both laced with a light chilli heat and a warm flavour from the allspice. I serve this with grilled chicken or steak, some refried beans (see page 63) and a few salads. It also makes a simple, elegant starter or a delicious taco filling.

Sit the cobs up in a bowl and scrape a knife down along each cob at a 45 degree angle to shave off the kernels into the bowl.

Heat the oil and butter in a pan over a medium heat and, when it is gently sizzling, add the onion, corn and chilli. Cook for at least 5 minutes or until the onion has turned translucent without colouring, before adding the garlic, allspice, salt and pepper. Turn up the heat and cook for another 5 to 10 minutes until the corn starts gently taking on some colour and caramelizing.

Pour over the lime juice, scatter with the fresh herbs and serve on small plates with generous spoonfuls of sour cream, a little grated cheese and a pinch of chilli powder. Eat with warm flat breads.

Warm courgette & corn salad
Add small, diced courgettes to the pan with the corn to create a warm courgette and corn salad, which is also delicious in quesadillas, tacos and burritos.

Fiery prawn &
mango salad

A spicy, nutty salad, full of the tastes of the Mexican
Caribbean, this is perfect for a starter or light lunch.

Preheat the oven to 150°C/300°F/gas 2. Rinse the wild rice
in cold water and drain in a colander. Heat the olive oil in a
saucepan and sweat the shallots over a medium heat,
seasoning with salt, pepper, cumin and oregano. Once they
are translucent, add the rice and stir-fry for a few minutes
before covering with the boiling stock. Simmer for about 25
minutes until most of the water is absorbed and the rice still
has some bite to it. Cover with butter papers or greaseproof
paper and a lid and cook in the oven for about 20 minutes.

Meanwhile, cover the couscous in 500ml boiling water, add
salt and pepper and let stand for 5 minutes. Fluff up with a
fork and drizzle with the extra virgin olive oil.

Put the nuts in a dry frying pan and cook over a medium
heat until they are lightly toasted. Roughly chop and add
to a large salad bowl. Toast the coconut in a dry frying pan
for about 5 minutes, stirring frequently, until golden. Pour
the oil into the frying pan and heat until it is shimmering.
Add the shallots and shallow fry them until they are crisp
and golden, trying not to burn them. Fish out with a slotted
spoon and drain on kitchen paper to absorb the oil. Mix the
toasted coconut and crisp-fried shallots and put into a
small serving bowl.

Heat the frying pan until searing hot, add the prawns and
toss them in a few tablespoons of the dressing for a minute,
just so that they absorb the flavours. Set aside.

Put the rice, couscous, mango, red onion, herbs, prawns and
radishes in the large salad bowl with the peanuts and toss
in the rest of the dressing. Serve with the small bowl of
chopped coriander, the crispy shallots and coconut and the
lime wedges.

Feeds 4

Preparation time:
35–40 minutes

200g wild rice (or pearled
   spelt)
2 tablespoons olive oil
2–3 shallots, finely chopped
sea salt and black pepper
½ teaspoon ground cumin
a good pinch of dried
   oregano
500ml chicken or vegetable
   stock (fresh or from a cube)
150g couscous
1 tablespoon extra virgin
   olive oil
80g peanuts
250g cooked, peeled prawns
1 x Caribbean chilli-citrus
   dressing (see page 80)
200g radishes, finely sliced
the flesh of 1 large mango or
   2 smaller ones, finely diced
½ large red onion, very
   finely diced
a large handful each of parsley,
   coriander and mint, chopped

To serve
60g grated fresh or
   desiccated coconut
100ml olive or vegetable oil
4 shallots, finely sliced
a small handful of
   chopped coriander leaves
lime wedges

Hot chorizo salad with butternut squash & baby tomatoes

Serves 4–6

Cooking time:
40 minutes

1 small butternut or onion
    squash, deseeded and cut
    roughly into 5cm pieces
1 chile de arbol or other dried
    chilli, chopped
1 teaspoon cumin seeds,
    ground
a small handful of oregano or
    marjoram, chopped
    (or 1 teaspoon dried)
vegetable or olive oil
sea salt and black pepper
2 red onions, roughly sliced
a small punnet of baby
    tomatoes
a small bunch of coriander,
    leaves, chopped
3–4 tablespoons extra
    virgin olive oil
4 large chorizo cooking
    sausages, casings removed
    and sausages bias cut into
    long rounds
150g cooked borlotti or
    pinto beans (see page 62)
a small bag of baby spinach
100g Pecorino cheese

This salad is packed full of flavour. Serve it as part of a spread or just as a hearty, deeply satisfying lunch dish.

Preheat the oven to 190°C/375°F/gas 5. Put the squash, chilli, cumin and oregano in a roasting dish with enough oil to coat lightly and season well with salt and pepper. Roast for about 15 minutes before adding the onion slices, turning to coat them in the oil. Roast for a further 10 minutes before adding the baby tomatoes and cooking for a final 10 minutes.

Meanwhile, pound the coriander leaves in a pestle and mortar with a pinch of salt until you have a green paste. Cover with the extra virgin olive oil and set aside.

Heat a griddle or frying pan over a medium to high heat and fry the chorizo for 2 to 3 minutes a side. Drain on kitchen paper. Gently mix the roasted vegetables and beans together in a large bowl with a tablespoon of the coriander oil and the spinach leaves. Divide the salad among four to six plates, adding pieces of the grilled chorizo. With a potato peeler, shave the Pecorino on top and drizzle with the coriander oil.

Pan-fried mackerel with a sweet-sour salad

Feeds 4

Preparation time:
35 minutes

½ white cabbage
1 sweet apple, peeled and
    cored
a small knob of butter
3 tablespoons currants
2 tablespoons pine nuts,
    toasted
a couple of large handfuls of
    rocket leaves
a baby gem lettuce
a handful of coriander leaves,
    roughly chopped
4 very fresh mackerel, filleted
sea salt and black pepper
1 tablespoon olive oil

For the dressing
1 tablespoon Chipotles en
    adobo (see page 36)
2 tablespoons sherry vinegar
1 teaspoon honey
sea salt and black pepper
120ml extra virgin olive oil

A love of sweet-sour flavours came to Veracruz from Sicily, via Spain and the invasion of Cortés. They are hard to resist.

Make the dressing by shaking all the ingredients together in a clean jam jar.

Shred the cabbage very finely with a mandolin or a sharp knife. The cabbage should be paper thin. Cube the apple, put into a large salad bowl with the cabbage and dress in a little of the dressing to stop the apple discolouring.

Heat the small knob of butter in a frying pan over a high heat, add the currants and, after about 30 seconds, add the pine nuts. Fry until the currants are puffed up. Allow to cool.

Wash the salad leaves, dry them and add them to the salad bowl with the coriander.

When you are ready to eat, season the mackerel fillets generously with salt and pepper on both sides. Heat the same frying pan over a high heat and when it is smoking hot, add the olive oil. Fry the mackerel skin-side down for a few minutes until the skin is crisp and golden, and then turn and cook on the other side for a few minutes more until the flesh turns from translucent to opaque.

Toss the salad in the rest of the dressing and serve with the pan-fried mackerel fillets.

Sweet & spicy pecan nut & goat's cheese salad

This salad combines the Mexican love of caramelized nuts with goat's cheese and pomegranate seeds. A salad to brighten up the winter months.

Preheat the oven to 180°C/350°F/gas 4. For the spiced nuts, gently heat the whole spices in a frying pan to release their flavours and grind to a powder in a pestle and mortar or spice grinder. Mix together with the other ingredients into a paste, adding the nuts last and making sure they are evenly coated. Lay the nuts on a lined baking tray and roast for about 10 to 15 minutes until slightly caramelized and golden. Allow to cool on the tray. These nuts can be stored in an airtight jar for several weeks.

Meanwhile, roll the pomegranate across the work surface, pressing down firmly with the palm of your hand to release all the seeds. Cut the fruit in half and empty out the juice and seeds into a bowl, picking out any of the white pith, which is bitter and horrible tasting. Strain the juice into a bowl, keeping the seeds for the salad.

To make the dressing, mix the pomegranate juice and the balsamic vinegar together with a pinch of salt and pepper, followed by the extra virgin olive oil.

In a large bowl, add the salad leaves, herbs, pomegranate seeds, nuts, a splash of the dressing and gently toss together. Crumble the goat's cheese on top and drizzle over a little more of the dressing so that the leaves glisten and look well dressed.

Serves 4

Preparation time:
25 minutes

1 pomegranate
2 tablespoons balsamic vinegar
sea salt and black pepper
70ml extra virgin olive oil
150g mixed leaves (rocket, mustard leaf, baby spinach)
2 bulbs of chicory, leaves separated
leaves from 1 small bunch of basil
1 tablespoon chives, chopped
100g goat's cheese

For the spiced nuts
1 teaspoon cumin seeds
3 cloves
8 allspice berries
¼ teaspoon coriander seeds
½ teaspoon sweet pimentón (smoked paprika)
½ teaspoon sea salt
a pinch of cayenne pepper
15g icing sugar
20ml olive oil
100g pecan nuts

CHAPTER 5

Street food

The king of Mexican street food is the taco.

This is not the crisp, rolled shell sold in Tex-Mex supper kits, but a soft-cooked flatbread that comes hot off the grill, impregnated with that enticing charred flavour that all things cooked over charcoal acquire. This chapter will show you how to make your own tortillas, how to eat a taco (no knives and forks allowed!), how to fold burritos and the rest ...

This type of food is about layering flavours. Each single ingredient might have a simple taste, like the earthiness of corn, the meatiness of beans, the tanginess of raw onion or the heat of a chilli salsa. Each of these single components will not immediately wow you, but the slow build up will result in a dish that assaults the taste buds. This food grips all the senses, whether it is the crunch of crisp lettuce, the smell of spiced meat, the soft yielding bite into corn or the sight of all the colours at play together on your plate.

Once you have mastered the essence of Mexican eating – piling delicious toppings of meat, fish and vegetables on a variety of different shapes and sizes of tortilla – you are half-way to understanding the relaxed, fun and hands-on approach to eating this country's delicious food. Scoop up your taco, half-rolled, half-folded, hot, messy and delicious ...

This is food to feast on and share.

Step 1. Mix the flour, salt and olive oil together in a bowl, add half the warm water and let sit for 10 minutes. Slowly add more water, little by little, kneading with your hands for about 5 minutes until a dough is formed. It should feel soft, slightly sticky and smooth. Cover with a damp cloth until you are ready to roll the tortillas.

Step 2. Roll a portion of the dough into a small ball, just bigger than a 50-pence piece. Place it on one half of the polythene bag and press the dough down to a flattish shape with your first two fingers. Cover with the second sheet of plastic (this stops the dough sticking) and roll out the dough or press in the tortilla press to a 1 to 2mm thickness. Too thick will not be great to eat, but if you roll the tortillas too thin, they are hard to handle. You should get a tortilla about 10cm in diameter.

How to make tortillas

There is nothing like the flavour of freshly grilled corn tortillas, the Mexican flat breads that transport food to your mouth in place of a fork or spoon. They are hard to find here, so below is a blissfully easy recipe to make them at home.

Makes about 20 tortillas
Preparation time: 15 minutes

450g masa harina or fine
  cornmeal (NOT white cornflour)

a good pinch of sea salt
2 tablespoons olive oil
600ml hand-hot water

Step 3. Heat a large, heavy-bottomed frying pan or flat griddle. Peel the tortilla from the polythene and carefully place in the dry pan. Cook until the tortilla changes colour and slightly puffs up. I like mine a little charred too. When it has taken a bit of colour on one side, turn it over and cook on the other side.

Step 4. Keep the cooked tortillas warm by wrapping them in a tea towel, napkin or foil and keeping them in a low oven as you cook the rest. There is nothing worse than a cold tortilla!

NOTE You will need a polythene food bag, torn into its two halves, and a rolling pin or tortilla press.

A taco for all seasons

Here are four delicious fillings for tacos, one for each season of the year. Serve your chosen filling in a warmed bowl with wedges of lime, chopped coriander, table salsas and hot tortillas from the oven. All recipes feed four people as a starter or eat with rice and/or beans for supper, allowing 4 or 5 small tacos per person or a couple of larger ones. Even better, eat like the Mexicans and serve along with a handful of other dishes for fun sharing. All these fillings are delicious on bruschetta, tostadas, quesadillas, and burritos.

Spring tacos with mushrooms

Cooking time:
15–20 minutes

25g butter
2 tablespoons olive oil
750g mixed mushrooms,
    sliced
sea salt and black pepper
1 tablespoon truffle oil
    (optional)
2 shallots, finely chopped
2 cloves of garlic, finely
    chopped
a small handful tarragon,
    chopped

To serve
a small handful of parsley,
    roughly chopped
grated Pecorino cheese
Addictive sweet chipotle
    paste (see page 38)

The Mexicans love wild mushrooms. In the spring, morels and St. George's mushrooms come out in Britain among other varieties. If you can get wild mushrooms, add some sliced to normal field mushrooms or include a little dried porcini for a real treat. This filling is also really delicious in quesadillas.

Heat half the butter and olive oil in a frying pan and add the mushrooms, seasoning with salt and pepper. Cook over a high heat until the mushrooms have released their juices and the juice has started to evaporate, about 10 minutes. Add the rest of the butter and the oil (including the truffle oil if you are using it), the shallots and garlic and cook until soft. Sprinkle with the tarragon and check the seasoning.

Spoon the mushrooms into a heated earthenware dish that will look fun on the table and sprinkle over the parsley and cheese. This is incredibly delicious with my sweet chipotle paste, but also yummy with the Fresh tomato salsa on page 26 and a dollop of crème fraîche.

Creamy mushroom tacos
For a creamier taco, add 200ml crème fraîche to the mushrooms when they are cooked and simmer for a few minutes.

Summer tacos with courgette & corn

I love this filling. Lightly sautéed courgette and corn flavoured with fresh summer herbs. What could be simpler?

Heat a heavy-bottomed frying pan and add the oil. When it is hot, add the shallots, garlic, corn, chilli and courgettes. Fry, stirring all the time, until the vegetables are gently coloured on all sides and the onion is translucent. It is delicious if the courgette still has a little bite. Stir in the herbs, squeeze over the limes and season to taste.

This is really good sprinkled with a little crumbled feta.

Summer tacos with chorizo
This taco filling is delicious with diced chorizo added with the vegetables.

Cooking time:
5 minutes

2 tablespoons olive or
    vegetable oil
2 small shallots, finely
    chopped
1 clove of garlic, chopped
corn kernels cut from a cob
1 green chilli, finely chopped
700g courgettes, cut into
    small dice
1 tablespoon chopped mint
1 tablespoon chopped chervil
juice of ½ lime
sea salt and black pepper
crumbled feta, to serve
    (optional)

Autumn tacos with onion squash & chorizo

Cooking time:
35 minutes

1 clove of garlic
sea salt and black pepper
4 tablespoons olive oil
about 1kg onion
  (or butternut) squash,
  deseeded and cut into
  2cm cubes
1 chile de arbol, finely
  chopped
4 (about 250g) chorizo
  cooking sausages, diced
2 shallots, finely chopped
1 tablespoon chopped
  oregano

The combination of sweet roasted squash and spicy, garlicky chorizo is unbeatable. This is one of my favourite taco fillings.

Preheat the oven to 200°C/400°F/gas 6. Smash the garlic with ½ teaspoon salt and mix in 3 tablespoons of the olive oil. Toss the squash in the garlicky oil in a roasting dish, sprinkle over the chilli and roast for 20 to 25 minutes until the squash is slightly blackened at the edges and soft.

Heat the remaining oil in a frying pan over a medium heat and add the chorizo and shallots. Sweat until the shallots have softened. Add the squash and oregano, stir and season with salt and pepper.

WHY NOT TRY
This filling is delicious topped with Pink pickled onions (see page 34), Fresh tomato salsa (see page 26) or simply chopped coriander and chives.

Winter tacos with creamy greens

For me, greens are quintessentially Mexican and different varieties are used in corn puddings, tacos and quesadillas. Play around with whatever is in season, whether it is chard, kale, greens or spinach. They are all delicious cooked in this light, creamy sauce.

Separate the leaves from the stalks, wash in a cold sink of water and finely shred. Put a pan of water on to boil and season well with salt. When it is boiling, add the greens and blanch for 5 minutes until the leaves have softened. Remove the leaves with a slotted spoon and now add the potatoes to the boiling water. Cook the potatoes for about 5 minutes until they are soft.

Meanwhile, heat the olive oil in a frying pan and cook the shallots, chilli and garlic over a medium heat until they have softened, seasoning well with salt and pepper. Add the greens and continue cooking for 5 minutes.

By this stage, the potatoes should be cooked. Drain them and add them to the greens with the crème fraîche, tarragon and white wine. Bring up to a simmer and cook gently for a few minutes so that the cream can reduce. Check for seasoning.

Serve the greens in a warm bowl at the table, sprinkled generously with grated Pecorino and add sliced radish.

Cooking time:
30 minutes

700g winter greens
sea salt and black pepper
500g potatoes, cut into
   small dice
2–3 tablespoons olive oil
2 shallots, finely chopped
1 jalapeño chilli,
   finely chopped
4 cloves of garlic,
   finely chopped
300ml crème fraîche
2 heaped tablespoons
   chopped tarragon
100ml white wine

To serve
grated Pecorino cheese
1 radish, sliced (optional)

Step 1. Arrange the table with delectable taco fillings, salsas and garnishes of your choice.

Step 2. Fill your taco with any of the fillings.

How to eat a taco

Eating tacos is the most fun. A basket perches on the table with a cloth inside, hiding slightly charred, hot tortillas (see page 100). These can be stuffed with your choice of fillings and spicy salsas. Be as inventive as you like with the fillings. Here are a few ideas to get you started ...

* sautéed courgette flowers
* chorizo with potatoes
* shredded chilli-smoked chicken

Step 3. Top with your favourite salsa, a sprinkling of chopped onion and coriander and a squeeze of lime.

Step 4. Eat with greed, gusto and glee.

* slow-cooked pork
* confit of pork
* poached and shredded chicken cooked in mouthwatering moles
* stuffed chillies
* beans gently cooked with spices and aromatics
* grilled fish

Spicy bird tacos

Feeds 4

Cooking time:
35 minutes

1–2 tablespoons olive oil
a small knob of butter
1 large onion, sliced
sea salt and black pepper
1 tablespoon brown sugar
a generous pinch of ground
  allspice
a generous pinch of
  ground cinammon
2 fresh bay leaves
2 fat cloves of garlic,
  chopped
2 x 400g tins of chopped
  tomatoes
2 tablespoons Chipotles
  en adobo (see page 36)
600–800g leftover chicken
  from a roast, shredded
16 small corn tortillas or
  8 larger ones

This spicy filling can be found at every street food stand in Mexico City. It is simple to make and can also be used to fill burritos, tortas, tamales, enchiladas, to top tostadas or even baked potatoes. It is a yummy recipe for using leftover chicken.

Heat the olive oil and butter in a pan and add the onion, salt, pepper, sugar, spices and bay leaves. Cook over a medium-high heat for 15 minutes, then add the garlic. Cook for a further 5 minutes.

Add the tomatoes and Chipotles and simmer for at least 15 minutes over a low heat – the longer the cooking, the better the taste. Finally, add the shredded chicken and season to taste.

Serve in a warm bowl at the table with bowls of rice and guacamole, sour cream, grated Lancashire or Cheshire cheese and the tortillas.

Totopos (tortilla chips)

Totopos, or chips as we call them, are leftover, stale tortillas (found in every Mexican kitchen), cut up into shapes, fried crisp and served still warm with everything from ceviches and seafood coctels to refried beans and sides of avocado. Of course you can buy tortilla chips at the supermarket, but these home-made ones are unbeatable.

Heat the vegetable oil in a large casserole or saucepan until it is shimmering hot.

Meanwhile, cut the tortillas into sixths, quarters or halves as is your want and test one in the hot oil. If the oil bubbles up vigorously, then it is up to temperature. If the oil doesn't move very much, wait for the temperature to rise further.

Fry the tortillas in batches so that you are not bringing the temperature of the oil down too much, until crisp and golden.

Alternatively, preheat the oven to 180°C/350°F/gas 4. Cut up the tortillas as above and, using a pastry brush, brush the tortilla pieces with oil. Bake on a baking tray for 10 to 15 minutes, moving them around so that they cook evenly during baking.

Sprinkle the chips with salt when still warm and serve with a fresh tomato salsa, guacamole, ceviche or refried beans.

NOTE You can leave the tortillas out overnight to get stale before frying. This will stop them absorbing so much oil.

You can also bake and fry flour tortillas, although they will not have the same flavour as corn and tend to absorb more oil.

Cooking time:
10–15 minutes

at least 1 litre
   vegetable oil
stale, home-made tortillas
   or bought corn tortillas
sea salt

A winning watermelon and tostada salad

Feeds 2

Cooking time:
5–10 minutes

1 large slice of watermelon
a handful of mixed seeds,
    such as pumpkin and
    sunflower
1 teaspoon sea salt
1 teaspoon hot chilli powder
1 teaspoon sugar
2 bought corn tortillas
    (a bit stale is fine)
vegetable or sunflower oil,
    for frying,
a large handful of mixed
    salad leaves
extra virgin olive oil
juice of ½ lime
100g mild crumbly cheese,
    like a fresh goat's cheese
    or, at a push, feta
2 tablespoons sour cream,
    thinned with a little milk

It is with great pleasure that I introduce the winning recipe from my online Mexican Food Made Simple competition held in August 2009.

Steve Gale takes the flavours and seasonings of Mexican street food to make an inventive and delicious salad. As he explains, 'The magic ingredient here is the chilli-salt-sugar mix. In Mexico, street hawkers pair ice-cold fruit with this salty-sweet tangy sprinkle that delivers a spicy, citrusy chilli hit. Just what you need on a roasting summer's day on the beach or in the city. It also works in grey Britain!'

Deseed and dice the watermelon into small cubes, about 1 to 2cm big.

In a dry frying pan, toast the seeds until golden, taking care not to burn them, and set aside to cool

In a pestle and mortar, grind together the salt, chilli and sugar.

In a frying pan, shallow-fry the tortillas in the oil one at a time over a medium heat until golden and crispy. This should take about 2 minutes on each side. Drain on kitchen paper and keep warm.

Now build the dish. Place a tortilla on a plate. In a bowl, dress the salad leaves with a little olive oil and a squeeze of lime juice and place a little on the fried tortilla. Artfully layer the watermelon, a crumble of the cheese and a sprinkle of seeds. Dust with a good pinch of the chilli salt, then go again for a second layer – you want some good height on the salad.

Dress with a drizzle of sour cream, another squeeze of lime juice and serve straight away – you want the tortilla to remain crispy and delicious.

Smoked mackerel tostadas

Serves 4

These tostadas are delicious, combining the smoky flavours of mackerel and chipotle and lightened with a vibrant, citrusy tomato salsa, then finished with a slice of creamy avocado and a sprinkling of deep-fried shallots.

To make the tostadas, cut out rounds of tortilla about 4 to 5cm across and fry or bake the rounds as in the Totopos recipe (see page 113) until crisp and golden.

To make the crispy shallots, pour the oil into the frying pan and heat until it is shimmering. Add the shallots and shallow fry them until they are crisp and golden, trying not to burn them. Fish out with a slotted spoon and drain on kitchen paper to absorb the oil.

Flake the smoked mackerel with a fork and mix into the fresh tomato salsa. Spread each tostada generously with chipotle mayonnaise and top with shredded lettuce. Spoon over the smoked mackerel salsa and top with a slice of avocado. Squeeze over a little lime juice and, if you like, sprinkle with deep-fried shallots.

NOTE This is delicious with any type of smoked fish and also with very fresh raw mackerel, cut as for sushi.

Preparation time:
10–15 minutes

4 large bought corn
   tortillas or 8 leftover
   home-made ones
300g smoked mackerel fillet
1 quantity of Fresh tomato
   salsa (see page 26)

For the deep-fried
   shallots (optional)
100ml olive or vegetable oil
4 shallots, finely sliced

To serve
Chipotle mayonnaise
   (see page 38)
1 cos lettuce, shredded
1 avocado, peeled and sliced
a few squeezes of lime juice

The tastiest black bean tostadas

Serves 4

Cooking time:
25–30 minutes

400g cooked black beans
    (see page 62), with the
    cooking liquid reserved
1 fat clove of garlic, crushed
1 shallot, finely chopped
juice of ½ lime
2 tablespoons extra virgin
    olive oil
sea salt and black pepper
a good pinch of ground cumin
vegetable oil
12–16 tostadas (see recipe on
    page 115)
100g feta cheese, crumbled
1–2 avocados, peeled, stoned
    and roughly sliced
cos lettuce, finely shredded
1 quantity Fresh tomato salsa
    (see page 26) or
    An incredible ancho relish
    (see page 34)

Black beans are so simple that somehow it is hard to imagine them tasting this good. This is a deeply satisfying starter or snack that you can rustle up in very little time.

Purée half the beans with the garlic, shallot, lime juice and a little splash of the olive oil in a food processor with enough of the bean liquid to loosen the blades. In a heavy-bottomed pan, heat a tablespoon of the olive oil, add the bean purée and the rest of the beans and stir gently for about 10 minutes until slightly thickened. Season with salt, pepper and a pinch of ground cumin and set aside.

Heat a frying pan filled with about 5cm of vegetable oil. When it is shimmering hot, add the tortillas, in small batches, and fry until crisp and golden. Remove from the pan and drain on kitchen paper.

Place the tortillas on a couple of serving plates if you are using small, home-made ones or on individual plates if you are using the larger, bought tortillas. Spread the beans on the tostadas. Top with the crumbled feta, avocado, shredded lettuce and finally the salsa or relish.

This is delicious with the Blow-your-head-off habanero salsa on page 30 or the addictive sweet chipotle paste on page 38. Or, why not try drizzled with a little sour cream.

Chicken and chipotle tostadas

This tostada is delicious with leftover chicken. Shred into small pieces and toss with a tablespoon or two of chipotle paste (see page 38). Grill or fry until golden and serve on top of the above tostadas, drizzled with a little sour cream.

Steak burritos

Skirt steak, a cheap cut over here because of its sinews, is a favoured piece of meat in Mexico thanks to its rich flavour. As long as you cook it quickly over a high heat, the meat will be tender and delicious. I cook whole steaks to stuff inside burritos and tacos, and then cut them up in slithers across the grain to get a soft, meaty texture.

If the skirt steak is cut into thick slices, butterfly it out into thin steaks by cutting it down the middle with a sharp knife. Marinate the steak in the olive oil, garlic, orange juice, chilli and seasoning for 30 minutes.

Heat each tortilla in a hot, dry frying pan for about 10 seconds a side to make it soft and pliable.

Heat up a griddle or heavy-bottomed frying pan until smoking hot and add the olive oil. Top the spring onions and peel off the outer skin before chopping them up into 2–3cm lengths. Season with salt and pepper and put onto the hot griddle.

Pat the steak dry with some kitchen paper and add to the griddle pan. Sear for a minute on each side (or 90 seconds, tops). Leave to stand for a minute on a warm plate whilst you finish cooking the spring onions. They should be soft and slightly charred. When the spring onions are cooked, remove from the pan, add the reserved marinade from the steak and let it sizzle up before pouring over the warm beans.

Chop up the steak into bite-size pieces across the grain (you can see the grain all running in one direction, so cut across these lines at a right angle).

Fill the tortillas (see steps on pages 118 and 119) with the steak, beans, rice, salsa and spring onions. Add some mashed avocado, a drizzle of crème fraîche, some coriander leaf and the cheese, and toast if you like your burrito crispy. Eat up at once.

Feeds 4

Cooking time:
10 minutes

For the steak
600g skirt steak
3–4 tablespoons olive oil
2 cloves of garlic, crushed
juice of ½ orange
1 chile de arbol, finely
  chopped
sea salt and black pepper

4 wraps (corn tortillas,
  chapattis or other wraps)
1 tablespoon olive oil
4 spring onions
about 150g warm cooked
  black beans (see page 62)
about 200g warm rice
  (optional)
1 quantity Roast chipotle
  salsa (see page 29)
1 avocado, peeled and
  mashed with the juice of
  a lime
3–4 tablespoons crème
  fraîche
chopped coriander leaves
120g extra mature Cheddar
  cheese (optional)

Step 1. Heat the tortilla in a hot, dry frying pan for about 10 seconds a side to make it soft and pliable.

Step 2. Spoon the filling into the middle of the burrito. Fill with rice or beans and drizzle with crème fraîche and salsa.

How to fold burritos

Burritos are to northern Mexico what pasties are to Cornwall. Traditionally, farm labourers would take out bundles of beans, rice and whatever else was in the kitchen, all wrapped up in flour tortillas to keep them going all day. You can fill burritos with practically any of the recipes in this book (see the list of fillings on pages 110–111 for inspiration). Hunt for the thinnest flour tortillas you can find – they make the best burritos.

Step 3. Fold over the outside edges of the tortilla and push the ingredients down to tame them a little.

Step 4. Roll over and, if you like, toast it again for a few minutes a side to get a toasted, crisp burrito.

Swiss chard tamales

Makes about 18

Cooking time:
2½–3 hours

300g lard, at room
    temperature
1½ teaspoons
    baking powder
2 teaspoons sea salt
500g tamale flour
625ml hot water
200ml cold chicken stock
    (fresh or from a cube)

For the filling
sea salt and black pepper
a large bunch (about 1.8kg)
    of Swiss chard
3 tablespoons olive oil
1 large white onion,
    finely sliced
3 cloves of garlic,
    finely chopped
1 jalapeño chilli, finely
    chopped
150ml white wine
a good pinch of ground
    allspice
100g Pecorino cheese,
    grated
a small handful of tarragon,
    chopped
400ml crème fraîche

Tamales are the most loved and revered street food snack in the whole of Mexico – small steamed corn dumplings, which are light, fluffy and totally irresistible. I fill them with vegetables and serve with a salad for lunch or alongside grilled lamb or steamed fish. Getting a friend or small person to help wrap the bundles will cut down on the work dramatically!

You will need a large steamer, some greaseproof paper and kitchen foil.

Prepare the filling. Bring a large pan of salted water to the boil. Cut the leaves away from the stalks of the Swiss chard and chop into fine ribbons. Thinly slice the stalks. Cook the Swiss chard stalks in the boiling water for about 7 to 10 minutes until they are tender, and the leaves for 3 to 4 minutes. Drain both thoroughly.

Heat the olive oil in a large pan and sweat the onion for 5 minutes before adding the garlic and chilli. Cook over a medium heat until the onion is translucent and completely soft. Add the chard leaves and stalks, white wine, allspice, Pecorino, tarragon and crème fraîche, season with salt and pepper and turn the heat up to reduce the cream to a thickish sauce to coat the chard. Check the seasoning – it should be yummy – and leave to cool.

Beat the lard, baking powder and salt together in a mixer with a dough hook or whisk for about 5 minutes until light, white and fluffy. Meanwhile, mix the tamale flour and hot water together with a wooden spoon. Add the tamale dough to the lard, bit by bit, until it is fully incorporated into the lard. Slowly beat in the stock.

To assemble the tamales, cut out about eighteen rectangles of both foil and greaseproof paper, measuring 20cm by 12cm. Cover two-thirds of a piece of greaseproof paper with a thin layer, about 3 to 4mm, of the tamale dough using a spatula or the back of a spoon. Put a heaped teaspoonful or small table-spoonful of the cooled Swiss chard filling in the middle of the dough and roll over so that the dough covers the filling completely (if you add too much filling it will leak out of the dough. Tuck up the bottom of the greaseproof paper and roll up in a piece of foil, folding over the bottom of the foil so that the bottom is sealed and the top is open. Repeat with all the tamales and then stand them up in a steamer, with the open end at the top. Steam for about 50 minutes until the dough comes away easily from the greaseproof paper. Eat with more of the leftover, warmed Swiss chard cream on the side of the tamales.

NOTE Buy the tamale flour from The Cool Chile Co. (see page 218) – it makes the lightest, fluffiest tamales imaginable. You can also use this same dough to make a shepherd's pie in place of mashed potato.

VARIATIONS
Feel free to experiment with sautéed courgette, blanched spring greens or cavolo nero or steamed broccoli, all cooked in the crème fraîche and Pecorino sauce. These tamales are also exquisite filled with shredded chicken in the mole sauce on page 42.

CHAPTER 6

Cheesy things

There are few cuisines where cheese is more appreciated than Mexican.

Quesadillas [kay-sah-dee-uh], from the Spanish meaning 'little cheesy things', are toasted or deep-fried tortillas filled with cheese and other ingredients. Hot, melting and exceedingly good, they are a staple snack on the streets, as are mouthwatering puff pastry empanadas. And for a sit-down treat, Queso fundido is the Mexican cheese fondue, oozing cheese heated in earthenware pots and topped with slow-braised meats or chorizo.

Thanks to thousands of farmers producing artisan cheeses from their own small cattle herds, the quality of Mexican cheese is incredible. But you don't have to import these specialist cheeses to cook 'authentic' Mexican food. The following can be used to great effect:

Ricotta has a tantalizing, delicate sweetness to it, which melts in the mouth when stuffed inside chillies and courgette flowers. Produced all over Mexico, it can be used as a substitute for the Mexican cheese requesón.

Mozzarella I use in place of queso Oaxaqueño, a famous string cheese from Oaxaca that has amazing melting qualities. Use a ball of fresh mozzarella in salads, or grated mozzarella melted inside quesadillas. Middle Eastern shops also stock a cheese that can be used called tressé.

I like to grate extra mature Cheddar (try Quick's, Keen's or Montgomery's) or a Lincolnshire Poacher (another delicious hard cheese) to mix with mozzarella and melt inside quesadillas and queso fundido. It adds a lovely rich taste.

Lancashire tastes very similar to a young queso fresco, which is crumbled over tacos and tostadas to give a fresh, curd flavour to your Mexican dishes.

Feta also tastes like queso fresco. I often soak a block of feta in water for 20 minutes and then crumble it in soups or on tacos to get the right, distinctive flavour.

Pecorino is very similar to queso añejo, a Mexican hard cheese. Its rich, salty flavour adds a wonderful layer of flavour and complexity.

If you feel happy when you are faced with a plate of cheeses, then Mexico is your country.

feta

pecorino

ricotta

mozzarella

cheddar

lancashire

3 ripe tomatoes
1 teaspoon olive oil
120g chorizo cooking
   sausages, casings removed
   and roughly chopped
½ white onion, finely diced
¼ teaspoon ground cumin
sea salt and black pepper
150g mozzarella, grated
150g mature Cheddar
   cheese, grated

To serve
warm tortillas

Queso fundido

The equivalent of our Welsh rarebit, this recipe comes from northern Mexico. I serve it in a terracotta baking dish with a basket full of warmed flour tortillas. It is mouthwateringly good comfort food.

Preheat the oven to 180°C/350°F/gas 4. Cover the tomatoes with boiling water and count to 20. Drain and pierce them with a knife so that the skins slip off easily. Scoop out the seeds and dice the flesh into small cubes.

Heat the olive oil in a heavy-bottomed saucepan and brown the chorizo over a medium heat, using a wooden spoon to break up the meat into small pieces. Add the onion and cumin to the pan and cook for 5 to 10 minutes until the onion is translucent. Add the tomatoes and cook until most of the moisture has evaporated from the pan and you have a mince-like texture. Season with salt and pepper.

Spread the mixture on to the bottom of a gratin dish so that it is just covering the bottom. Cover with the grated cheeses and put in the oven for about 10 minutes until the cheese is melted and bubbling or, if you prefer, stick under a hot grill.

Eat immediately with hot tortillas and a green salad. It is also rather good with the Simple roast chilli salsa on page 28.

Queso fundido with mushrooms
Replace the chorizo with the sautéed mushrooms from the steak recipe on page 154 for a delicious vegetarian alternative.

Herby ricotta dip

Serves 6

Fresh requesón, or ricotta, is made locally all over Mexico. I love it served simply with masses of chopped herbs, salt and pepper and scooped up with some freshly fried or baked tortilla chips (see page 113). It makes a fun, unusual dip before lunch or supper.

Whip the ricotta and goat's cheese together until soft and creamy. Mix in the Parmesan, lemon zest, olive oil and herbs. Taste and season with salt and pepper. Serve with summer vegetables or Totopos.

Chipotle ricotta dip

Mix together 300g fresh ricotta, a handful of chopped mint, a touch of honey, 2 cloves of crushed garlic and a heaped tablespoon of the Addictive sweet chipotle paste (see page 38) and season well with salt and pepper. Add the juice of a lime and stir well. This is delicious as a dip, on tostadas, bruschetta or crostini or it's yummy with roast aubergine, fennel and tomatoes.

Preparation time:
20 minutes

100g ricotta
100g goat's cheese
30g Parmesan cheese,
  grated
zest of 1 lemon
50ml extra virgin olive oil
1 tablespoon chopped
  tarragon
1 tablespoon chopped
  flat-leaf parsley
1 tablespoon
  chopped chervil
1 tablespoon
  chopped chives
sea salt and black pepper

Step 1. Cut the potatoes in equal-size chunks and fry until tender. Leave them to cool a little and then cut them into 1cm dice. Cook the onion until soft, add the garlic and cook for a further 3 minutes. Mix in the chorizo and potato, turn up the heat and fry for another 5 minutes. Mix in the thyme and season. Assemble all the rest of the quesadilla ingredients.

Step 2. Spread a quarter of the chorizo mixture on one half of a tortilla and sprinkle with a fistful of cheese.

Chorizo, potato & thyme quesadillas

Quesadillas [kay-sa-dee-yas], stuffed with melted cheese and anything else you fancy, are good at any time of the day. but particularly in front of a movie or the big match.

Enough for 4 large quesadillas
Cooking time: 20 minutes

350g potatoes
½ onion, finely chopped
1 clove of garlic, chopped

200g chorizo cooking sausage, chopped
a small bunch of thyme, chopped
sea salt and black pepper
4 large flour or corn tortillas
400g cheese, grated
olive oil

Step 3. Fold the tortilla over so that you have a half moon. Brush it with a little olive oil (so the tortilla doesn't stick to the pan) and place in a hot, dry frying pan or griddle and cook until golden and crisp. Repeat with the remaining tortillas.

Step 4. Cut into wedges and serve with your favourite table salsa.

NOTE I find that a mix of extra mature English Cheddar and a little grated mozzarella makes the perfect cheese mix, with a good flavour and the right gooiness.

Classic mushroom quesadillas

Cooking time:
20 minutes

2–3 tablespoons olive oil
4 portobello mushrooms,
    chopped
sea salt and black pepper
3 baby shallots,
    finely chopped
2 cloves of garlic,
    finely chopped
2 tablespoons roughly
    chopped flat-leaf parsley
zest of ½ lemon
4 large corn or flour tortillas
400g cheese, grated
olive oil

For a real treat, add a drizzle of truffle oil to mimic the flavour of huitlacoche, a delectable fungus that grows on corn in Mexico.

Heat half the oil in a frying pan and add the mushrooms, seasoning with salt and pepper. Cook over a high heat until the mushrooms have released their juices and the juice has started to evaporate. At this stage, add the rest of the oil and the shallots and cook until soft. Add the garlic and cook for a further 3 minutes, by which stage the mushrooms should be soft too.

Mix in the chopped parsley and lemon zest and spread some of the mixture on to one half of a tortilla. Sprinkle over a quarter of the cheese.

Fold the tortilla over so that you have a half moon. Brush it with a little olive oil (so the tortilla doesn't stick to the pan) and place in a hot, dry frying pan or griddle and cook until golden and crisp (see method on page 129).

Cut into wedges and serve with your favourite table salsa.

VARIATIONS
Fill your quesadillas with:
Courgette flowers, onion and garlic
Spicy chicken taco filling (see page 112)
Swiss chard tamale filling (see page 120–1)
Courgette and corn (see page 105)

Or try with any leftovers nestling in your fridge.

Deep-fried black bean quesadillas

These deep-fried quesadillas are created using home-made corn dough. Fry until crisp and golden, and serve with a simple green salad and your favourite salsa. Scrumptious.

Make the dough according to the instructions on page 100–101. Mix the beans and cheeses in a bowl with the chipotle, coriander and spring onions, it will look a terrible mess! Season with salt and pepper.

Roll out balls of dough (see method on page 100) into small 10cm circles. Keeping the circle on the sheet of plastic, pick it up in your hand and spread one half with the bean mix, leaving a little border of white dough around the edge. On no account let greed grab a hold of you and be tempted to overfill it, as I tend to do, it will only burst open when fried. Carefully fold over the plastic so that you are pressing the corn quesadilla together into a half moon shape. Through the plastic (so that the dough doesn't stick to your hands) pinch the edges of the quesadilla together so that it seals.

Lay out the quesadilla on a baking sheet dusted with the flour and carry on until you have used up all the dough and filling. Meanwhile, place a casserole over a high heat and fill with the oil (you can reuse it by straining when it is cool and storing in a dark, dry place). Test the oil with a shred of corn and if the oil bubbles up energetically, it is up to heat (about 180°C).

Add a few quesadillas at a time so as not to bring down the temperature of the oil and make the quesadillas too greasy, and fry until crisp and golden. These can then be kept in a warm oven for a few hours until you are ready to eat, although they are best eaten as soon as possible.

Serves 4 as a starter

Cooking time:
40 minutes

½ quantity corn tortilla dough
  (see page 100–101)
200g Frijoles refritos (refried
  beans) (see page 63)
100g mature Cheddar cheese,
  grated
50g mozzarella, grated
1 teaspoon Chipotle purée
  (see page 37)
a small handful of coriander
  leaves
2 spring onions, finely
  chopped
sea salt and black pepper
fine polenta or plain flour,
  for dusting
about 2 litres sunflower
  or groundnut oil

Cheese & courgette filo parcels

Makes 6 parcels

Cooking time:
25 minutes

50g butter, melted
60g mozzarella, grated
35g cream cheese
1 courgette, grated and
   squeezed dry
1 tablespoon each
   chopped basil and chervil
sea salt and black pepper
4 sheets of filo pastry

These oozing, cheesy courgette parcels are stunning when served alongside the Minty courgette soup on page 69.

Preheat the oven to 180°C/350°F/gas 4. Line and grease a baking tray with a little of the melted butter. Mix the cheeses, courgette and herbs together and season to taste.

Work with two sheets of filo pastry at a time made into a double layer, keeping the rest covered under a damp cloth. Brush the melted butter over the sheets of filo and cut lengthways into three strips, approximately 8cm wide.

Place a heaped teaspoon of the cheese mixture at one end of each strip. Form a triangle by folding the right hand corner over the mixture to the opposite side, then continue to fold, using up the entire length of the pastry.

Brush all over with butter and place on the baking tray with the seam side down. Continue with the remaining pastry to make 6 parcels, then bake for 25 minutes or until golden.

Ham & cheese empanadas

Empanadas are a flaky, rough pastry filled with any of the usual street food fillings and baked until puffed up, golden and crispy. I came across a very glamorous 80-year-old woman selling these in a riverside town in Veracruz. She made around 500 a day.

Preheat the oven to 200°C/400°F/gas 6. Line a couple of baking trays with non-stick baking paper. Mix the mayonnaise with the mustard, chillies and Tabasco and season to taste. Stir in the Cheddar and ham.

Flour a surface and roll out the pastry to about a 3 to 4mm thickness. Cut out eight circles, 12cm wide. Spread a small teaspoonful of the ham mixture on the base of each circle, making sure you leave a 1cm border. Lightly brush the edges with a little of the beaten egg, fold over the empty half of the circle and, with a fork, crimp the edge of each empanada to secure and seal them. Brush the empanadas with beaten egg and gently make a few air holes in each one with a sharp knife or fork.

Place on the baking trays and cook for 10 minutes, then lower the oven temperature to 180°C/350°F/gas 4 and cook for a further 10 minutes or until golden. Eat at once!

NOTE The empanadas can be deep-fried if you prefer.

Makes 8–10 empanadas

Cooking time:
30 minutes

3 tablespoons mayonnaise
1 teaspoon Dijon mustard
1–2 green chillies,
   finely diced
a little splash of Tabasco
   sauce
sea salt and black pepper
200g Cheddar cheese,
   grated
150g ham, roughly chopped
   or torn into strips
1 packet of puff pastry
1 egg, beaten

Tlayudas (Oaxacan pizzas)

Serves 4

Cooking time:
15 minutes

1 large bag of baby spinach
small knob of butter
sea salt and black pepper
olive oil
4 large flat breads (large
    Middle Eastern pittas,
    Turkish or Italian
    flat breads)
4 heaped tablespoons
    Guacamole (see page 48) or
    the flesh of a ripe avocado
2 balls of mozzarella, grated
80g Pecorino or mature
    Cheddar cheese, grated
300g leftover chicken or
    2 chicken breasts, poached
    and shredded (see
    page 140)
8 sun blushed tomatoes
    or very ripe fresh
    tomatoes, sliced
2 tablespoons roughly
    chopped herbs (basil,
    tarragon, chervil or
    coriander)
2 handfuls of rocket

Tlayudas [clae-yoo-das] are wonderfully messy open pizzas, sold at night on the streets of Oaxaca. Try them grilled, fried or baked in the oven.

Wash the spinach and shake dry. Heat a large pan, add the butter to it, then add the spinach and cook for a few minutes until the spinach has wilted down. Remove from the pan, squeeze dry and season with salt, pepper and a drizzle of olive oil.

Heat a large frying pan big enough to hold the flat breads or a flat griddle pan. Put one flat bread in the pan and sprinkle with a tiny bit of water to gently heat it. Once slightly crisp, turn it over. Spread a layer of guacamole on first, followed by some grated mozzarella and a quarter of the rest of the ingredients. When the outer side of the bread is crisp and the mozzarella has begun to melt, fold the pizza over so it looks a little like an open calzone. Slide on to a plate and slice into pieces.

Serve the tlayuda with the Blow-your-head-off habanaro salsa (see page 30) or the Roast tomato sauce (see page 30), with or without chipotles.

VARIATIONS
You can fill these Oaxacan pizzas with anything you like, from grilled chorizo and strips of skirt steak to fish and grilled seasonal vegetables.

Simply delicious ricotta-stuffed courgette flowers

Serves 4

Cooking time:
35–40 minutes

250g ricotta
12 courgette flowers, with
    baby courgettes attached
4 tablespoons extra virgin
    olive oil
2 shallots, finely chopped
1 clove of garlic, crushed
zest of 1 lemon
2 tablespoons finely chopped
    tarragon leaves,
½ teaspoon local honey
sea salt and black pepper

To serve
2 cloves of garlic, sliced
a small bag of rocket leaves
a little extra virgin olive oil
a little grated Pecorino
    cheese (or Parmesan)
juice of ½ lemon

These are a real treat and very easy to make.

Put the ricotta in a piece of muslin or fine cloth and squeeze into a tight ball to wring out any excess liquid. Leave to drip over a bowl.

Meanwhile, wipe the courgette flowers clean with a slightly damp, clean kitchen cloth and break off the baby courgettes. Slice the courgettes in half lengthways. Carefully make a slit down one side of each flower by peeling apart two petals away from each other. Pinch out the stamen from inside the flower.

Heat 2 tablespoons of the olive oil very gently in a pan and add the shallots and crushed garlic. Cook very gently until soft and then add the ricotta, lemon zest, tarragon and honey. Season well with salt and pepper and stir over the low heat for 5 minutes.

Stuff each ricotta flower with a little teaspoon of the ricotta mixture. It is very tempting to overstuff them, but they will only burst open when you cook them later. Press the petals together and twist around slightly to close up the ends.

Heat another tablespoon of oil in a frying pan until gently bubbling and add half the courgette flowers, sautéing on all sides until slightly coloured. Drain on kitchen paper and repeat with the remaining flowers. Set aside in a warm place.

Heat the remaining oil in the pan and when very hot, add the courgette halves and sliced garlic and sauté over a high heat for a few minutes until the vegetables are both starting to colour. Toss the rocket with the olive oil, Pecorino, lemon juice and salt and pepper. Top with the courgettes and serve with three courgette flowers to a plate.

Smoky stuffed peppers

Serves 4

This is a delicious recipe with rich goat's cheese, smoky chillies and sweet mangoes. Heavenly as a starter or serve it with rice for a main course, perhaps with refried beans.

Preheat the oven to 200°C/400°F/gas 6. Cut the potatoes to equal-size chunks and cook until tender. Drain, leave them to cool a little and then cut them into tiny 1cm cubes.

Meanwhile, slice the peppers in half and remove the seeds. Heat the olive oil in a wide, heavy-bottomed pan and add the shallots. Sweat for about 5 minutes, or until the shallots are turning translucent, before adding the garlic and mango. Cook for another 5 minutes, seasoning well with salt and pepper, then add the goat's cheese, Chipotles, balsamic vinegar and oregano. Continue cooking, breaking up the mango and chipotle so that they both become absorbed in the sauce, for about 5 minutes. Add the wine and potatoes, stir and cook over a low heat for 5 minutes. Check for seasoning.

Fill each pepper half with some of the filling and place in a large baking tray with a splash of water in the bottom. Bake in the oven for about 30 minutes or until the peppers are soft and the filling is hot and golden. Sprinkle them with the Pecorino and bake for a further 5 minutes, then eat up at once.

NOTE It is much easier to peel a shallot if you first dip it briefly in piping hot water.

VARIATIONS
These are also delicious stuffed with the Picadillo on page 151, just a simple filling of refried beans and grated cheese, or the courgette and corn filling on page 105. You could also add 100g finely diced cooking chorizo to the onions.

Smoky stuffed chillies
Stuff ancho chillies instead of red peppers by soaking them in simmering water flavoured with 2 tablespoons of red wine vinegar and a tablespoon of demerara sugar until soft. Make a slit, remove the seeds and stuff with the filling above.

Cooking time:
about 1 hour

600g potatoes, peeled
4 red peppers
2 tablespoons olive oil
5 shallots, finely chopped
4 cloves of garlic, chopped
2 small ripe mangoes,
    flesh diced (I like the
    honey ones)
sea salt and black pepper
150g soft goat's cheese
1 heaped tablespoon
    Chipotles en adobo
    (see page 36)
1 teaspoon good quality
    balsamic vinegar
a small handful of oregano,
    finely chopped
120ml white wine
60g Pecorino cheese, grated

CHAPTER 7

Slow-cooked
main courses

Slow cooking
is at the heart of Mexican street food,

where meltingly tender meat and fish are shredded and added to chilli, tomato or herb sauces, then spooned into tacos, on top of tostadas or used as fillings for chillies, tamales, enchiladas, quesadillas and burritos. If you have leftovers from any joint, this is a neat way to use them up. Chop up the meat and add it to one of the recipes in this chapter, and soon you will find that you are cooking like a Mexican.

Braising is such a brilliant way to cook cheaper cuts because fat from the meat breaks down into the simmering broth, which you can drain or skim off later. This kind of slow cooking also softens tough sinews, producing a gentle, soft and yielding meat. Meatballs are another way of using up the tougher cuts of pork and beef by first grinding them, and then baking in simmering chilli-spiked sauces.

Sauces for this style of cooking are flavoured with spices such as cinnamon, allspice or cloves and spiked with the flavours of fresh and dried chillies. Moles are similarly spiced, but with the addition of ground nuts and dried fruit and the occasional slab of dark chocolate to add depth to the overall flavour.

If all this sounds a little heavy, bowls of finely diced red onions, chopped coriander, shredded cabbage, radishes and fresh salsas are handed round at the table to offset the rich, meaty, unctuous flavours. All that is then needed is a bowl of steaming rice, some hot tortillas and an icy cold beer or tequila.

The joy of lazy, gentle cooking in a fast-paced world.

Poaching and braising, Mexican style

Poaching and braising were fairly new to me when I first got to Mexico, but I now find these methods indispensable to my cooking. Essentially, the meat is gently simmered until it is tender enough to fall apart, at which point it is served in soft, yielding pieces on rice or corn, or shredded and cooked in any number of Mexican sauces and moles to ladle into tacos, on to tostadas, stuff inside chillies or fill enchiladas. Once you have got to grips with how easy it is, you will be putting everything in a pot and leaving it to do its thing.

Poaches 1 chicken

Cooking time:
30–40 minutes

1 medium-sized
   free-range chicken
3 sprigs of tarragon or
   flat-leaf parsley (or both)
a small bunch of thyme
   (optional)
½ onion
10 peppercorns
1 carrot, roughly chopped
a few bay leaves

To poach a chicken

Place the chicken in a large pot with the other ingredients and cover with water. Put over a medium heat, cover and bring to the boil. Once boiling, turn the heat right down so that the water is very gently simmering, occasionally breaking bubbles on the surface. Simmer for about 15 to 20 minutes and then turn off the heat.

Leave the chicken to cool in the broth with the lid on, where it will carry on gently cooking, leaving you with a tender bird. When the chicken is cool, you can remove it from the broth, reserving the poaching liquid (it is now a light chicken stock) for soups or sauces.

Braising meat

To braise meat, use cheap cuts like shoulder, belly, shin, cheek or brisket and either leave them whole or cut them into quarters. Cover at least a third of the way up with water, stock, wine or a marinade. Cook over a very low heat, covered tightly so that no steam escapes and the liquid barely breaks a bubble. Braise, for 3 or 4 hours until the meat is soft and falling apart, perfect for shredding and marinating. Alternatively, braise cheap cuts in the oven at about 140°C/275°F/gas 1 for several hours.

Chicken & chorizo in an almond mole

Serves 6

Cooking time:
1 hour

5 plum tomatoes
½ large Spanish onion
4 cloves of garlic
60g raisins
1 tablespoon oil or lard
70g blanched almonds
50g stale white country
  bread, torn into pieces
1 ancho chilli or a Spanish
  dried red chilli
2 sprigs each of thyme,
  oregano and marjoram
1 small bunch of
  flat-leaf parsley
50g sesame seeds
2 cloves
4 black peppercorns
1 x 4cm cinnamon stick
450ml chicken stock or
  poaching liquid
2 teaspoons tomato purée
1 tablespoon Chipotle purée
  (optional) (see page 37)
sea salt and black pepper
8 small chorizo cooking
  sausages, casings removed
  and cut in half
1 tablespoon olive oil
50g green Spanish olives,
  roughly chopped
20g salted capers, washed
  and chopped
1 poached chicken
  (see page 140), shredded

This is a simple take on a classic Mexican recipe. The chicken is gently poached (see page 140), and then shredded and added to a simple mole.

Heat a large frying pan over a medium heat and dry roast the tomatoes, onion and garlic cloves (see method on page 28). When the skins of the tomatoes are black and blistered, remove all the ingredients and put in a blender.

In the same frying pan, sauté the raisins in the oil or lard for 2 minutes until they have puffed up, then remove from the pan. Fry the almonds for 2 minutes until golden and remove. Fry the bread with the chilli and herbs until golden, then remove from the pan. Finally, fry the sesame seeds until golden.

Grind the spices in a pestle and mortar or spice grinder. Add all these ingredients to the blender with 200ml of the chicken stock and the tomato and chipotle purées. Blend to a purée. Taste and season.

Fry the chorizo in the olive oil until cooked through. Add the puréed mixture and cook for 5 minutes. Add a further 250ml of the stock, the olives, capers and shredded chicken and heat through.

Meatballs de Mehico!

Feeds 6

I love meatballs and cooked in Smoky tomato sauce (page 32) they are a real treat.

Preheat the oven to 180°/350°F/gas 4. Whiz the onion and garlic in a food processor until finely chopped and squidge into the minced meat in a large mixing bowl (I always use my hands for this as it is so much easier). Gently mix in the rest of the ingredients apart from the milk, rice and tomato sauce adding the boiled eggs last and seasoning with salt and pepper. If you want, you can fry a little bit of the mixture to check the seasoning.

Add the milk and rice. The mixture will be quite soft but don't worry, just put it in the fridge for 10 minutes to firm up, and then start rolling the mince mixture into balls about 3 to 4cm in diameter. Once again, let them rest in the fridge until you are ready with the sauce.

Place the balls in a baking dish, pour over the tomato sauce (which should be quite liquid, so stir through some water or stock if it looks too thick) and cover with foil. Bake for about 45 minutes until the meatballs are cooked through. Serve with rice or on egg noodles.

Cooking time:
1 hour 15 minutes

1 small white onion
3 cloves of garlic
250g lean minced beef
250g minced pork
50g stale breadcrumbs
1 tablespoon chopped
   flat-leaf parsley
1 tablespoon chopped mint
1 teaspoon ground cumin
½ teaspoon ground allspice
2 teaspoons tomato purée
½ teaspoon mustard
a good splash of
   Worcestershire sauce
1 egg, lightly beaten
1 heaped tablespoon capers,
   rinsed and chopped
2 hard-boiled eggs, peeled
   and roughly chopped
sea salt and black pepper
180ml milk
150g long-grain rice
1 quantity Smoky tomato
   sauce (see page 32)

An easy, speedy chile con carne

Feeds 6–8

Cooking time:
3½ hours

1kg beef, cut into 4 pieces
  (use stewing steak, silver
  side or another cheap cut)
3 onions
4 cloves of garlic
olive oil
300g spicy cooking chorizo,
  cut into chunks
2 teaspoons each of ground
  cumin and allspice
1 teaspoon cloves
1 large cinnamon stick
3 bay leaves
2 tablespoons chopped
  fresh oregano or
  2 teaspoons dried
2 ancho chillies, deseeded
2 chiles de arbol
2 teaspoons sea salt
black pepper
3 tablespoons cider or
  balsamic vinegar
2 x 400g tins plum tomatoes
2 tablespoons tomato
  ketchup
2 tablespoons muscovado
  or dark brown sugar
2 x 400g tins borlotti beans,
  drained or 600g cooked
  (see page 62)

Rich, warming and comforting, chile con carne may not be Mexican but it is such a favourite recipe that I had to include it in here. This recipe is gently spiced so ramp up the chillies if you like it hot.

Preheat the oven to 120°C/225°F/gas 1. Take the meat out of the fridge to de-chill. Pulse the onions and garlic in a food processor until finely chopped. Heat 2 tablespoons olive oil in a large casserole and sear the meat on all sides until golden. Set to one side and add another small slug of oil to brown the chorizo. Remove and add the onion and garlic, spices, herbs and chillies then cook until soft in the chorizo oil. Season with salt and pepper and add the vinegar, tomatoes, ketchup and sugar.

Put all the meat back into the pot with 400ml water (or red wine if you prefer), bring up to a simmer and cook, covered, in the low oven. After 2 hours, check the meat and add the beans. Cook for a further hour and just before serving, pull the meat apart with a pair of forks.

NOTE The joy of this recipe is that it takes half as long to prepare as most other chile con carnes. By quickly searing a few, large chunks of beef you skip that horrendously boring job of browning batches of mince and avoid the risk of stewing the meat instead of caramelising it. It is fast and easy and the meat gently braises in the oven until it is soft enough to pull apart (see page 140 on braising).

WHY NOT TRY
Serve with a Fresh tomato salsa (see page 26), grated cheese, sour cream and simple cabbage salad.

Feeds 8

Cooking time:
30 minutes prep +
4 hours braising

1 quantity Delicious meat
    marinade (see page 33)
approx 1.8kg shoulder
    of lamb or mutton
½ bottle medium-
    bodied red wine
4–5 tomatoes, roughly
    chopped
8 large floury potatoes

For the cabbage and
radish salad
¾ white cabbage
a bunch of radishes tops
    removed
½ red onion, finely sliced
a handful of coriander leaves,
    chopped
extra virgin olive oil
sea salt and black pepper
1–2 tablespoons
    sherry vinegar

To serve
Chile de arbol salsa
    (see page 26)
2 limes, quartered

Barbacoa

Barbacoa is slow-cooked meat; a recipe for high days and holidays in Mexico. This is my version, a rich, exotically spiced dish that melts in the mouth. Cook this with mutton, if you can get hold of it, as the flavour is even more delicious than lamb.

Make the marinade the day before you want to cook, put it into a plastic bag with the meat and store it in the fridge overnight (check there are no holes or you will get into a real mess – double wrapping is sometimes a safe bet).

The following day, put the lamb, marinade, wine and tomatoes into a large pan and cover with water. Put a pierced piece of clingfilm and a tight-fitting lid on the pan so that none of the liquid can evaporate, bring to a simmer and cook over a low, gentle heat (so that the liquid is barely breaking a bubble).

After 3 hours, remove the clingfilm and add the potatoes so that they have time to cook in the broth. Cook for about another hour until the meat is completely tender and the potatoes are cooked. Remove the lamb and potatoes from the broth and whiz it up with a stick blender.

When you want to eat, make the cabbage and radish salad by slicing the cabbage very, very finely with a sharp knife or mandolin so that the slices are almost transparent. Cut the radishes in the same way (they can be kept in icy water in the fridge and made a few hours ahead). Toss the cabbage, radish, onion and coriander in a drizzle of extra virgin olive oil with salt and pepper and the sherry vinegar.

Bring the lamb up to heat and serve in deep bowls, surrounded by the potatoes and the broth and with a handful of the bright salad on top. Drizzle a little of the red-hot salsa on the salad with a squeeze of lime juice.

NOTE The meat can be cooked the day before you want to eat and stored in the fridge to allow the flavours to develop.

Tamarind & chilli-infused belly of pork

Feeds 6

Part-cook this recipe the day before. The prep takes about 15 minutes and the next day you will be rewarded with a feast.

The day before just put the pork belly in a pan that is just big enough to comfortably fit the joint. Cover in cold water and bring to the boil. Discard the water (which will contain impurities and excess fat) and rinse out the pan.

Smash the garlic cloves once with the flat side of a knife and add to the pan with the pork, spices, onion, tamarind, chipotle, coriander, soy sauce, half the vinegar and sugar and enough water to cover. Bring to the boil and simmer gently over a low heat for about 1½ hours until the meat is tender, topping up with more boiling water if you need to.

Remove the meat from the pan and remove the bones from the joint as they come out very easily and make carving a doddle. Put the pork in the fridge, skin side up and uncovered, so that the meat dries out (to give you the best crackling).

Meanwhile, simmer the poaching juices with the rest of the sugar and balsamic vinegar for about 20 to 25 minutes until the liquid has reduced to a syrupy juice. Transfer this gravy to a bowl, cool and store in the fridge until needed.

The next day, rub the joint in a tablespoon of olive oil, sea salt and black pepper. Preheat the oven to 180°C/350°F/gas 4 and roast the joint for 20 minutes before turning the oven up to 230°C/450°F/gas 8 and roasting until the crackling has turned crisp and golden. Watch out, as the crackling can turn quickly from golden brown to black. Meanwhile, skim and discard the fat from the gravy you made the day before and heat up. Serve slices of the pork on rice, soft polenta, mashed potatoes or sautéed greens

Cooking time:
4 hours (best part-cooked the day before)

approx 2kg pork belly
   Ask your butcher to score the skin of the pork belly, or do it yourself with a Stanley knife, making a criss-cross pattern across the skin.
8 cloves of garlic
2 cinnamon sticks, broken in half
1 teaspoon cloves
1 teaspoon allspice berries
1 onion
1 tablespoon concentrated tamarind paste
1 heaped tablespoon Chipotle purée (see page 37)
a small handful of fresh coriander (inc. roots if possible)
4 tablespoons soy sauce
4 tablespoons good quality balsamic vinegar
6 tablespoons demerara sugar
olive or vegetable oil
sea salt and black pepper

Red snapper with tomatoes & pineapple

Feeds 6

Cooking time:
50 minutes

80ml extra virgin olive oil
1 onion, finely chopped
½ pineapple, peeled, cored
    and cut into 5mm cubes
1 bulb of fennel,
    finely chopped
3 sticks of celery,
    finely chopped
a good pinch of demerara
    sugar
1 chile de arbol, or fresh
    red chilli, deseeded and
    finely chopped (optional)
600g cherry tomatoes,
    quartered
1 large handful of chervil
    and marjoram, chopped
3 tablespoons Pernod
    (or absinthe)
juice and zest of 1 lemon
sea salt and black pepper
1 piece of red snapper
    (or use sea bass or sea
    trout), weighing
    about 1.5kg

If you think, like me, that ham and pineapple pizza is the devil's food, then you might reckon this sounds a strange recipe. However, question not and cook away. The combination of the sweet pineapple and tomato, the citrus and the fresh herbs makes a delightful summer dish.

Preheat the oven to 200°C/400°F/gas 6. Heat half the olive oil in a pan over a low heat and add the onion, pineapple, fennel, celery, sugar and chilli, if using. Sweat gently for 5 to 10 minutes until the vegetables turn translucent. Add the tomatoes, herbs, Pernod and zest and juice of the lemon and cook for a further 10 minutes, seasoning well with salt and pepper.

Place the fish inside a double-layered piece of foil and season generously, outside and in, with salt and pepper. Drizzle the tomato mixture with the rest of the olive oil and stuff half of it inside the fish and half on top. Wrap the foil around the fish to seal completely and roast in the oven for 20 to 25 minutes until the flesh just comes away from the bone. Serve with masses of new potatoes tossed in lots of butter.

Rainbow trout baked with chilli cream

Feeds 4

This chilli cream is known as rajas [ra-haas] in Mexico. It has a soft, creamy and slightly spicy flavour that is delicious over baked fish. I love the sauce so much that I use it in all sorts of other dishes (try it over roast chicken). It takes no time to make.

Preheat the oven to 190°C/375°F/gas 5. Bake the peppers in the hot oven for 10 to 15 minutes until blackened and blistered. Put them in a bowl, cover with clingfilm and set aside for 15 minutes.

Meanwhile, heat the olive oil in a frying pan, add the onion and chillies and sauté for 10 minutes until the onion is translucent. Add the garlic and cook for a few more minutes, seasoning with salt and pepper. Peel and deseed the green peppers, slice into thin strips and add to the onion and chilli mixture. Stir in the crème fraîche and check for seasoning.

Meanwhile, season the trout inside and out with salt and pepper and, if you have it, add the thyme to the belly. Wrap the trout in foil, adding the white wine to the parcel and a drizzle of olive oil. Bake the fish in the oven for 15 to 20 minutes or until the flesh comes away easily from the bones.

Fillet the fish and pour over the warm sauce. This is delicious with boiled, buttered potatoes or rice.

Broccoli or cauliflower with chilli cream

I like to pour this sauce over steamed broccoli or cauliflower, sprinkle with Pecorino and heat through under a grill or in the oven until golden brown.

Cooking time:
1 hour

2 large green peppers or
  poblano chillies
1–2 tablespoons olive oil
½ large onion, sliced
3 fresh green chillies,
  deseeded and sliced
  (serranos or jalapeños
  would be perfect)
2 cloves of garlic, sliced
sea salt and black pepper
250ml double cream or
  crème fraîche
2 rainbow trout, gutted
a few sprigs of thyme
½ cup white wine

One-pot bacon, beans & pumpkin

Cooking time:
50 minutes plus soaking
overnight

160g dried pinto beans
2 tablespoons olive oil
200g pancetta, diced
1 white onion, sliced
3 cloves of garlic, finely
chopped
1/2 teaspoon ground cumin
500g pumpkin, peeled and
diced
2 red peppers, deseeded and
sliced
2 teaspoons Chipotle purée
(see page 36)
2 bay leaves
5 sprigs of oregano
200g baby tomatoes
500ml chicken stock

To serve
100ml sour cream
40g pumpkin seeds
    toased
a small handful chopped
    coriander

This is rich, warming comfort food – easy to prepare,
and lovely with the Green rice (see page 64).

Soak the pinto beans in cold water overnight.

Preheat the oven to 180°C/350°F/gas 4. Heat the olive oil in
a heavy-bottomed pan, add the pancetta and cook until
slightly golden. Add the onion, garlic and cumin and cook
for a further 5 minutes before adding the pumpkin, pepper,
chipotle, herbs and baby tomatoes. Cook until everything
has slightly softened, then add the beans and the stock.

Cover with baking parchment and a lid and place in the
oven or carry on cooking on the stove for about 45 minutes
until the beans are soft.

Serve with the sour cream, pumpkin seeds and the fresh
coriander.

Picadillo

This sweet-savoury recipe is great on its own with rice, stuffed inside tamales, burritos or chillies (particularly ancho and chipotle) or served as a pasta sauce. Yummy.

Mix the meats together in a bowl, season and set aside.

For the roast tomato sauce, roast the tomatoes, onion, pepper, chillies and garlic in a large, dry frying pan until they are blistered, blackened and softened all over. The garlic and chillies will be ready at least 5 minutes before the onion, pepper and tomatoes, so remove them as they are cooked. Cool slightly, then peel away the skin from all the vegetables, remove the seeds from the chilli if you wish, and roughly purée the vegetables in a food processor.

In a large, heavy-bottomed saucepan, heat the olive oil and add the puréed sauce, cooking for a few minutes over a high heat. Turn the heat right down and season generously with salt and pepper. Simmer gently for 15 to 20 minutes, stirring regularly, until the mixture has reduced and slightly thickened.

In a large non-stick frying pan, heat another 2 tablespoons of olive oil and add the meat bit by bit, seasoning as you cook and breaking up any lumps with a wooden spoon, until well browned. Sprinkle the cinnamon, cumin, cloves, olives and raisins over the meat and stir well. Transfer the meat mixture to a large casserole, pour over the tomato sauce and stock and bring to a gentle simmer. Cook over the lowest heat, stirring occasionally, until nearly all the liquid has evaporated.

Add the toasted almonds. Taste, add a little of the vinegar, and taste again. The vinegar brings out all the flavours, but you must be careful not to add too much. Season with salt and pepper. The finished picadillo should not be too wet.

The picadillo tastes better if left for a day or two in the fridge, reheated and served with all the usual accompaniments – guacamole, salsa, sour cream, grated cheese and tortillas.

Cooking time:
1½ hours

250g minced beef
250g minced pork
sea salt and black pepper
2 tablespoons olive oil
½ teaspoon ground
  cinnamon
½ teaspoon ground cumin
½ teaspoon ground cloves
50g pimento-stuffed green
  olives, roughly chopped
70g raisins
250ml beef stock
50g slivered almonds,
  toasted
1 tablespoon red
  wine vinegar

For the roast tomato sauce
7 plum tomatoes
1 onion, chopped
1 red pepper, deseeded
  and chopped
3 jalapeño chillies
2 cloves of garlic
2 tablespoons olive oil
sea salt and black pepper

CHAPTER 8

From the grill

Grilling is fast cooking,
and an essential
part of Mexican street food.

Add flavour to meat beforehand with simple marinades and spice rubs or add it afterwards by spooning over freshly made salsas.

This type of cooking is made for long, lazy afternoons surrounded by friends, where the food is so quick to cook that it becomes part of the entertainment of the day. Invite friends early and give one person responsibility for the drinks and put someone else in charge of making the fresh, scorching salsas. Have your rice ready in the oven, salads prepared and cooking tongs for the best grillers so that they can take part in their own cook-off.

Sit back with ice-cold drinks
or a good wine and forget about the
world for an hour or two.

Rib-eye steak with chilli mushrooms

Feeds 4

Cooking time:
30–35 minutes

4 rib-eye steaks
25g butter
750g mixed mushrooms, sliced
sea salt and black pepper
olive oil
5 shallots, finely sliced
1 chile de arbol, finely chopped (see page 24)
4 cloves of garlic, finely chopped
1 heaped teaspoon Chipotle purée (see page 37)
a small handful of coriander and tarragon leaves, chopped

Grilled steak seems made for these sautéed mushrooms. I cook this for really special occasions.

Take the steaks out of the fridge at least 30 minutes before you are ready to eat so that they can reach room temperature.

Heat a large, heavy frying pan over a high heat, add a knob of the butter and the mushrooms and season with salt and pepper. Cook for about 10 minutes, by which time the mushrooms will have leached a lot of juices, which will slowly evaporate off, producing an intense mushroom flavour.

In a separate pan, add a few tablespoons of the olive oil and sweat the shallots and chilli over a medium heat until the shallots turn translucent. Add the garlic and cook for another few minutes before adding the mushrooms, about 100ml water and the Chipotle purée. Cook for another 10 minutes over a low heat.

When you are ready to eat, heat the large, heavy frying pan or a griddle pan until it is smoking hot and season the steaks generously with salt and pepper on both sides. Add a knob of the butter and a splash of olive oil to the pan and cook the steaks for a few minutes a side (depending on their thickness and how you like them cooked) and then leave to rest in a warm place for 10 minutes.

Add the chopped herbs to the mushrooms and serve with the steaks, some spuds and a fresh green salad.

NOTE I like to use a combination of flat mushrooms and any wild mushrooms that happen to be in season.

Torta (the Mexican club sandwich)

Makes 4

Preparation time: :
20 minutes

2 large, ripe tomatoes or
  Fresh tomato salsa
  (see page 14)
sea salt and black pepper
1 red chilli, finely chopped
a drizzle of olive oil
300g cooking chorizo
4 ciabatta buns
1 tablespoon lard or olive oil
  (optional)
8 large tablespoons
  refried beans (see page 63)
1 avocado, mashed with the
  juice of ½ lime
½ red onion,
  sliced very thinly
1–2 baby gem lettuces
4 very generous tablespoons
  Chipotle mayonnaise
  (see page 39) or ordinary
  mayonnaise

Mention the word 'torta' to any *chilango* (someone who comes from Mexico City) and you will see a faraway look come over them as they are transported back to the torta stands that line the streets of the capital. This sandwich is not for the faint-hearted, but it is exceedingly good.

Slice the tomatoes and dress them in salt and pepper, the chilli and a drizzle of olive oil.

Slice the chorizo up into bite-size pieces that can easily be grilled, unless you are cooking them outside on the barbecue, in which case grill the sausages first and then slice them so you don't lose precious pieces in the fire. Heat a griddle or frying pan until smoking hot, add the chorizo and cook for a few minutes a side until it is looking good and crispy. Remove to a plate and cut the buns in half. Brush both sides of the buns with the chorizo fat and a little extra lard or oil if you think they need it. Toast on the grill pan on both sides.

Smear one half of the buns with refried beans and top with the avocado, red onion, tomato, chorizo and lettuce. Smear the other half in the mayonnaise and press down firmly. Eat at once, preferably doused with healthy amounts of the blow-your-head-off habanero salsa on page 30 or the Fiery roast tomato salsa on page 159.

Chicken torta
Use leftover chicken (the BBQ'd chicken leftovers from page 160 are especially good) in the torta instead of chorizo, or try steak, pork or fish.

Vegetarian torta
Layer the sandwich up with grilled courgettes, mushrooms (see the taco filling on page 102) or grilled corn, sliced from the cob.

Grilled lamb chops with chilli jam

Feeds 4

Cooking time:
a few hours for jam +
about 10 minutes for the chops

For the tomato and chilli jam
½ tablespoon cumin seeds
1 tablespoon coriander seeds
½ tablespoon cloves
1 tablespoon allspice berries
½ tablespoon peppercorns
2 small cinnamon sticks
2.5kg tomatoes,
    roughly chopped
2 white onions,
    roughly chopped
4 cloves of garlic, finely
    chopped
3 habanero (Scotch bonnet)
    chillies, finely diced
a good pinch of chilli flakes
    (optional)
15g sea salt
250ml cider vinegar
juice of 2 limes
300g demerara sugar

For the chops
8 lamb cutlets
juice of 1 lemon
2 tablespoons olive oil
5 sprigs of oregano or
    marjoram
a pinch of ground cumin
sea salt and black pepper
1 large bag of baby spinach
    leaves, washed
crème fraîche (optional)

This chilli jam is delicious not only with grilled lamb chops but also with Cheddar cheese, sausages, in a marinade or to sweeten and liven up a gravy. Store in sterilized jars and it will keep for months in the fridge.

To make the jam, first wash 3 or 4 jam jars in very hot, soapy water, rinse and arrange on a baking sheet in a warm oven (100°C) to dry out. This process will sterilize the jars.

Tie the spices in some muslin or a square of J-cloth. Put all the ingredients except the sugar into a large pot and bring to the boil. Boil for 30 minutes, stirring from time to time. Add the sugar and continue to boil for a further hour, stirring regularly. Bottle at once in the hot, sterilized jars.

Place the lamb cutlets in a dish with the lemon juice, olive oil, oregano, cumin, salt and pepper and leave to marinate for at least 20 minutes.

Preheat a griddle pan, grill or large frying pan and grill the cutlets for 3 to 4 minutes a side or until cooked to your liking – I think they are delicious served pink.

Warm the spinach leaves in a pan with a drop of olive oil, salt and pepper for a minute until slightly wilted. Put a spoonful of spinach on each plate and top with two lamb cutlets and a heaped tablespoonful of the spicy chilli jam (and a dollop of crème fraîche if you are feeling wicked).

NOTE This recipe makes about 1 litre of jam.

Spicy spatchcock salad

Serves 6 (or a greedy 4)

If you are going to barbecue a bird, spatchcocking is an excellent way to go about it ensuring an evenly grilled, delicious specimen. Ask your butcher to do the spatchcocking or try it yourself (see below).

Preheat the oven to 180°C/350°F/gas 4. To spatchcock the bird, take a pair of sturdy scissors and cut along the length of the backbone on both sides to cut out. Now place the bird on a chopping board and press down sharply and firmly onto the breastbone so that the bird flattens out. Season well.

Lightly toast the spices in a dry frying pan and grind with the chilli to a coarse powder in a pestle and mortar or spice grinder. Add the olive oil, marjoram, lemon zest and garlic and once bashed to a paste, massage into the skin of the chicken and place in a plastic bag (with no holes). Leave to marinate overnight or for at least a few hours.

Remove the chicken from the fridge half an hour before cooking to bring up to room temperature. Heat a griddle pan or barbecue and brown the chicken on the skin side until golden, then turn for 6 to 8 minutes a side.

Place the torn pieces of bread in a roasting dish and toss with enough olive oil to coat each piece lightly. Season with salt and pepper. Put the chicken in the same dish and bake for about 15 minutes so that the croutons are golden and crisp and the chicken finishes cooking, keeping an eye on the croutons.

Meanwhile, sauté the currants in a hot frying pan with a splash of olive oil until they are puffed up and golden. Remove and repeat with the almonds, toasting them to a golden brown. Mix the vinegar, olive oil, salt and pepper in a jam jar.

When the chicken and croutons are done, remove from the roasting dish, swirl half the dressing in the pan to deglaze and pour over the salad leaves. Scatter in the currants, almonds and croutons and top with carved hunks of the chicken.

Cooking time:
1 hour

1 medium-sized free-range
   chicken
sea salt and black pepper
2 tablespoons cumin seeds
6 whole allspice
1 small cinnamon stick
1 chile de arbol,
   finely chopped
2 tablespoons olive oil
5 sprigs of marjoram,
   roughly chopped
zest of 1 lemon
4 cloves of garlic,
   roughly chopped

For the salad and dressing
½ loaf of rustic,
   country white bread,
   torn into bite-size pieces
olive oil
sea salt and black pepper
4 tablespoons currants,
   soaked in a splash of
   boiling water and a
   splash of sherry
40g almonds, chopped into
   thin slices
2 tablespoons sherry vinegar
4 tablespoons extra
   virgin olive oil
2 heads of chicory, separated
   and washed
1 bag of rocket leaves,
   washed

Chicken adobado (marinated chicken)

Feeds 4

Cooking time:
15 minutes +
overnight marinating

For the marinade
4 tablespoons olive oil
1 onion, chopped
8 cloves of garlic, chopped
4 heaped tablespoons
   tomato purée
juice of 2 oranges
45ml red wine vinegar
2 chiles de arbol,
   finely chopped
1 tablespoon Chipotle purée
   (see page 37)
a heaped handful of coriander
30ml soy sauce
1 tablespoon chopped fresh
   oregano or 1 teaspoon dried
30g brown sugar
1 tablespoon Worcestershire
   sauce
a few teaspoons of sea salt
   and some black pepper

1 medium-sized free-range
   chicken, segmented or 12
   chicken bits
1 x Pink pickled onion
   (see page 34)

This is the easiest marinade in the world and makes for a devilishly good chicken recipe that is smoky, sweet, hot and aromatic. It is just as easy to chargrill indoors in the winter as to barbecue outside in the summer.

Whiz all the marinade ingredients together in a blender and pour over the chicken bits. Marinate overnight or for at least a few hours in the fridge. Remove the chicken from the fridge at least half an hour before cooking to allow it to come to room temperature.

Preheat a griddle pan until smoking hot or light charcoals on the barbecue and wait until they have died down enough so that you can hold your hand a hand's length over the fire and count to five without squealing. Once this is ready, grill the chicken bits until nicely coloured on each side and still moist in the middle (about 6 minutes a side, depending on the cut). If I am cooking the chicken inside, I griddle until crispy and golden on each side before finishing in a medium oven (180°C) for 5 minutes to minimize smoking out the house.

Serve with the Pink pickled onion (see page 34), some refried beans (see page 63) and a green salad.

Barbecued monkfish with a blow-your-head-off salsa

Serves 6

This is a simple recipe to cook on the barbecue.

Cut the monkfish tail lengthways down the middle and cut each half into three equal-size pieces. It is a very dense fish so will be much easier to cook in steaks. Put the monkfish in a shallow bowl, season well with salt and pepper, drizzle with the olive oil and lime juice and scatter with the bay leaves. Coat the monkfish pieces well and leave in the fridge to marinate for at least 1 hour.

Light the barbecue at least an hour before you want to eat and when the flames have died down and you can hold your hand a hand's length above the coals for 5 seconds, you are ready to cook.

Grill the fish for 3 to 5 minutes a side, depending on their thickness, basting with a little of the habanero salsa as you are cooking. Serve the fish with more sauce on the side, some refried beans (see page 63) or garlicky roast potatoes. It is also delicious with the chickpea salad on page 84.

NOTE This recipe can be cooked just as easily on a griddle pan.

WHY NOT TRY
I love to serve this with refried beans and the Mango & strawberry salad (see page 194) for pudding for a really fun lunch.

Cooking time:
10 minutes +
1 hour marinating

500g monkfish tail
sea salt and black pepper
2–3 tablespoons extra
  virgin olive oil
juice of ½ lime
5 fresh bay leaves, torn up
  into small pieces.
1 quantity blow-your-head-
  off salsa (see page 30)

A picnicky sardine escabeche

Serves 6–8

Cooking time:
30 minutes +
30 minutes infusing

10 sardines, cleaned and
   filleted
4 tablespoons coarse polenta
4–5 tablespoons olive oil
100g pine nuts, toasted
chopped flat-leaf parsley,
   to garnish

For the escabeche
4–5 tablespoons extra
   virgin olive oil
2 large red onions, sliced into
   thick wedges
75g currants
3 cloves of garlic, finely sliced
3 carrots, peeled and finely
   sliced
2 green chillies, sliced
2 tablespoons chopped
   marjoram, (or thyme or
   oregano)
2 bay leaves
1 cinnamon stick
5 allspice berries
300ml chicken stock
   (the better the quality, the
   better the escabeche)
100ml cider vinegar
180ml white wine or sherry
sea salt and black pepper
a good pinch of brown sugar
8 radishes, tops removed and
   finely sliced

Light and pretty and with an addictive balance of sweet-sour flavours, escabeche makes a perfect starter or lunch. This dish originated in Sicily and travelled to Mexico via Cortés and his band of conquistadors. It is incredibly easy to make and can be put together in advance.

To make the escabeche, pour the extra virgin olive oil into a hot frying pan and cook the onion, currants and garlic for a few minutes. Add the carrot, chillies, marjoram, bay leaves and spices and carry on cooking until the carrot takes on a little colour and the currants are puffed up and golden.

Pour in the stock, cider vinegar and wine and bring to the boil. Reduce the heat and simmer briskly for around 5 minutes for the flavours to combine. Season with salt, pepper and a good pinch of brown sugar, if you think it needs it, and add the radishes.

While the sauce is cooking, prepare the sardines. Dust the sardine fillets in seasoned polenta. Heat 2 to 3 tablespoons of the olive oil in a large, non-stick frying pan and cook the sardine fillets in two or three batches for just 1 to 2 minutes on each side until they have a lovely golden crust, adding extra oil if necessary. Drain on kitchen paper and transfer to a shallow dish.

Spoon the escabeche over the sardine fillets and leave to infuse for half an hour.

Sprinkle with the pine nuts and chopped parsley just before serving and have lots of crusty bread around to mop up the deliciously piquant juices.

Chilli prawns

Feeds 6

Cooking time:
30 minutes +
marinating time

3 ancho chillies (optional)
a head of garlic, broken up
   into cloves
1 onion
1–2 bay leaves (fresh
   if possible)
100g Chipotles en adobo
   (see page 36), plus extra
   for serving
100ml olive oil
30 large raw prawns (check
   they are sustainably
   caught)

To serve
warm tortillas
lime wedges
chopped coriander

In the upmarket restaurants of Mexico's larger cities, these prawns might be served on Griddled corn cakes (see page 180), whilst in villages they would always be wrapped in hot corn tortillas that have come straight off the comal.

If you are using ancho chillies, tear out the stems and seeds, cover with boiling water and simmer for 10 to 15 minutes until they are completely soft.

Peel the garlic cloves by smashing them with a pestle or heavy rolling pin and peeling off the papery skins.

Put the onion, bay leaves and 50ml water in a food processor and whiz into a smooth purée, adding the ancho chillies and Chipotles halfway through.

Heat the olive oil in a pan over a medium-high heat until it is shimmering hot, and then add the purée, stirring constantly, so that the chillies don't burn. Once you have 'fried' the purée for a few minutes, turn the heat down a little and continue to cook for another 5 to 10 minutes until the sauce has thickened a little. Cool.

When you are ready to eat, light a barbecue or heat a griddle pan and toss the prawns in the chilli marinade. If you like, you can leave the prawns to marinate for an hour or two or use immediately. Cook for a few minutes a side until the prawns have turned from grey to pink. Smear them with a touch more adobo and serve at once with the warm tortillas, lime wedges and some chopped coriander.

WHY NOT TRY
This is delicious served with the warm courgette and corn taco filling on page 105 and a crusty baguette.

Veracruzan grilled sea bass

Feeds 4–6

With tangy capers and olives, fiery jalapeños and a sweet tomato sauce, this recipe originates in Veracruz, where Cortés first landed in the Americas. It has all the tastes of the Mediterranean and is a lovely example of how flavours travel across the globe.

Preheat the oven to 190°C/375°F/gas 5.

Season the sea bass with plenty of salt and pepper, both inside the cavities and outside. Place in a double layer of kitchen foil and stuff the cavities with the herbs and lime slices. Drizzle with the olive oil and wine and bake for about 20 minutes or until the flesh comes easily away from the bones.

Serve the fish with the warm tomato sauce on the side and some steamed rice.

Cooking time:
20 minutes

2 whole sea bass, gutted
sea salt and black pepper
3–4 sprigs of fresh thyme
3–4 sprigs of fresh parsley
1 lime, thinly sliced
2 tablespoons extra virgin
   olive oil
100ml white wine
1 quantity of Tangy olive
   and caper tomato sauce
   (see page 31)

Griddled langoustines with coriander & pumpkin seed mole

Feeds 4

Cooking time:
20–25 minutes

20–24 langoustines
60g pumpkin seeds
2 chiles de arbol, finely
  chopped
1 habanero (Scotch bonnet)
  chilli, deseeded and
  finely chopped
2 cloves of garlic, bashed
  and peeled
2 large handfuls of coriander
  leaves, roughly chopped
1 handful each of chervil
  and mint leaves, chopped
200ml extra virgin olive oil
juice of 3 limes
4 spring onions, finely
  chopped
20g Pecorino cheese,
  grated

This is more like a sauce masquerading as a mole and far easier than all the other moles to make. It is glorious with langoustines, griddled scallops or fried fish. I also love it mixed with mayonnaise to dress a cold chicken and lettuce salad.

If you like, ask your fishmonger to split the langoustines open down the middle so that the flesh is easier to get out after they are cooked.

Toast the pumpkin seeds in a dry frying pan over a high heat for a few minutes or until they turn a pale golden colour and start to pop out of the pan. Transfer them to an upright food blender or pestle and mortar and grind them to a fine paste. Add the chillies and garlic and grind them into the pumpkin seed paste.

Now add the rest of the ingredients, apart from the langoustines, to the purée and blitz to a smooth paste.

Heat a large griddle pan or wok over a very high heat until it is smoking hot. Add the langoustines and several good dollops of the pumpkin seed paste. Griddle for 2 to 3 minutes a side until the paste is going golden brown and the langoustines have turned pink and are cooked through.

Serve with lime wedges and lots of crusty bread so that you can mop up all the sauce.

CHAPTER 9

Soul food

One of my favourite aspects of Mexican eating is the unpretentious home cooking.

The Mexicans are the kings of leftovers and any tiny bit of cheese, scrap of cream, leftover mince or meat will be reinvented in burritos, casseroles and pies. For the ubiquitous enchiladas, stale tortillas are blanched briefly in oil and dipped into red tomato or green tomatillo sauces, wrapped around leftover chicken or vegetables and baked in the oven. They are eaten steaming hot, drizzled with crema, sprinkled with grated cheese and served with bowls of salsa and chopped coriander at the table.

An even more popular 'leftovers' dish is chilaquiles. Stale tortillas are cut into chips and fried, then covered in tomato and chilli sauces and baked in the oven, perhaps with leftover shredded chicken, until piping hot. These types of corn dishes are warm, rich and comforting.

For breakfast, Huevos rancheros is a real soul food classic (see page 174), ritually eaten in the morning or, more often than not, the afternoon after big nights out. You need it after partying with Mexicans. My other favourite is the fried eggs they pop on top of a tomato sauce and lard-soaked tortilla, flavoured with masses of fresh tarragon (or hoja santa if you are in Mexico).

Lastly, no chapter on comfort food would be complete without a recipe for Fideus seco, golden-fried noodles baked in a rich tomato broth (see page 178). These are so soft they slip silkily down the throat. With crab, they make a very chi-chi dinner-party starter or main course, but I recommend cooking them without the crab for a simple supper guaranteed to keep any man, woman or child smiling, happy and on side!

A fast and delicious black pudding polenta

Feeds 6–8

Cooking time:
40–45 minutes

250g black pudding
2 tablespoons dripping,
    bacon fat or lard
1 onion, finely chopped
2 cloves of garlic,
    finely chopped
1 x 400g tin tomatoes
1 cinnamon stick, broken in
    half (or ½ teaspoon ground
    cinnamon)
a good pinch of ground
    allspice
1 tablespoon Chipotles
    en abobo (see page 36)
sea salt and black pepper
a small handful of
    chopped tarragon leaves
a good pinch of demerara
    sugar (optional)
80g chorizo salami, sliced
    into thin rounds
a handful of chopped parsley,
    to serve

For the polenta
1 teaspoon sea salt
200g quick-cook polenta
50g butter
2 tablespoons extra virgin
    olive oil
60g Pecorino cheese, grated
sea salt and black pepper

This is a delicious, meaty supper that is easy to cook and deeply satisfying. Soft polenta tastes very similar to the white corn that is cooked into tamales, the steamed dumplings that are a firm street food favourite. The flavour of corn seems to be a perfect match for black pudding, another very popular product from the revered pig.

Remove and discard the casing of the black pudding and cut up into rough slices. Melt the dripping in a large, heavy-bottomed frying pan over a medium heat and add the onion. Sweat for 10 minutes until the onion has turned translucent without colouring. Add the garlic and cook for another few minutes before adding the black pudding. Using a wooden spoon, break up the black pudding, getting rid of any lumps. It should dissolve with the heat into a mince. Cook over the heat for 5 minutes before adding the tomatoes, cinnamon stick, allspice and the Chipotles. Season with salt, pepper, tarragon and the sugar, if it needs it, and cook for about 10 minutes over a low heat.

When you are ready to eat, fry the chorizo slices until they are crisp and put 1 litre of water on to boil in a large pan, adding 1 teaspoon of the salt. When the water is boiling, pour in the polenta, stirring furiously with a whisk or wooden spoon to break up any lumps. Quick-cook polenta will be ready in a few minutes, so have your plates heated and the table set. Add the butter, olive oil and Pecorino and keep stirring, seasoning with plenty of black pepper and a touch of salt if it needs it (remembering that you have salted the water).

Serve spoonfuls of the black pudding on spoonfuls of the polenta and top with a disc of crisp-fried chorizo and a scattering of parsley.

Grilled polenta with mushrooms & greens

Feeds 4–6

The flavour of toasted corn, sautéed mushrooms and greens with a hint of chilli, takes me right back to the street food stalls of Mexico. This is a simple, healthy but delicious supper that is incredibly simple to pull together.

Put 750ml water on to boil in a large pan, adding the teaspoon of salt. When the water is boiling, pour in the polenta, stirring furiously with a whisk or wooden spoon to break up any lumps. Quick-cook polenta will be ready in a few minutes. Add the butter and 40g of the Pecorino and keep stirring, seasoning with plenty of black pepper and a touch of salt if it needs it (remembering that you have salted the water). Pour the polenta out onto a greased baking tray so it is 3 to 4cm thick. Cover with clingfilm and leave to set.

Heat a heavy-bottomed frying pan over a medium heat. Add a knob of the butter and the mushrooms, seasoning them well with salt and pepper. Cook for about 10 minutes, by which time the juices will have been released and then will gently simmer off.

Meanwhile, cut the broccoli stem into thin batons like French frites and cut the florets into small slices. Steam over simmering water until tender. Add the oil to another pan with another knob of butter and add the shallots. Sweat gently for 5 to 10 minutes until the shallots are soft and translucent without being coloured. Add the garlic and cook for another few minutes before adding the broccoli, thyme, chilli and mushrooms. Cook for 5 minutes until the broccoli is coming apart, then add the tarragon.

Cut long wedges of the polenta and grill under a hot grill until golden. Put on plates with the broccoli spooned over, drizzle with your best extra virgin olive oil and sprinkle with the remaining Pecorino.

Cooking time:
45 minutes

For the polenta
1 teaspoon sea salt
150g quick-cook polenta
40g butter
75g Pecorino cheese, grated
sea salt and black pepper

60g butter
500g mixed mushrooms, sliced
sea salt and black pepper
300g broccoli, purple sprouting or otherwise
1 tablespoon olive oil
4 small shallots, finely sliced
4 cloves of garlic, chopped
a small handful each of chopped thyme and tarragon leaves
1 chile de arbol, finely chopped
extra virgin olive oil

The great Mexican breakfast

Feeds 4

Cooking time:
50 minutes

For the tomato sauce
5–6 tablespoons lard or
    dripping
1 large onion, finely chopped
1–2 red chillies,
    finely chopped
3 cloves of garlic, chopped
2 tins plums tomatoes
sea salt and black pepper
1 teaspoon piloncillo or
    demerara sugar
a generous few splashes
    of Worcestershire sauce
a small handful of
    chopped tarragon

4 corn tortillas, chapattis
    or other flat breads
4 eggs
60g Lancashire cheese

This is a delicious, dead easy brunch that will cure any hangover, restore good moods and pep you up for the weekend. Put the tomato sauce on when you first wake up and leave it to simmer while you drink coffee and work up an appetite. Serve with refried beans for absolute perfection.

First, get the tomato sauce cooking. Heat 2 tablespoons of the lard in a wide saucepan and add the onion and chilli. Let them sweat over a low heat for 10 minutes until the onion is translucent. Add the garlic, cook for a few minutes more, and then add the tomatoes. Season the sauce well with salt, pepper, sugar and Worcestershire sauce, breaking up the tomatoes with a wooden spoon to make a roughly textured sauce. Leave the tomatoes to gently cook over a low heat for half an hour, adding a little water if they get too dry.

When you are ready to eat, melt 1 to 2 tablespoons of the lard in a frying pan and gently turn the flat breads in the fat. Put them in a low oven, wrapped in foil, to keep warm, along with four plates. Add the tarragon to the sauce and stir.

Melt the rest of the lard in the frying pan and turn the heat right up until the fat is sizzling. Fry the eggs, two at a time, spooning the lard over the top of them so that they turn a golden colour at the edges and absorb some of the flavour. Season the eggs well with salt and pepper.

Put a flat bread on each plate and top with the tomato sauce. Put a fried egg on top and scatter with the grated Lancashire cheese.

WHY NOT TRY
This is delicious with the Roast tomato salsa on page 30 or the sweet chipotle paste on page 38 and, for a serious breakfast, the refried beans on page 63.

Mexican scrambled eggs with chorizo

Feeds 5–6

Cooking time:
25 minutes

2-3 tablespoons olive oil
1 white onion, finely chopped
200g cooking chorizo,
   cut into 5mm chunks
1–2 fresh red chillies,
   deseeded and finely
   chopped
3–4 fat cloves of garlic,
   finely chopped
2 plum tomatoes, quartered
12 eggs
50ml whole milk
100g Pecorino or Lancashire
   cheese, grated
sea salt and black pepper
a large handful of coriander
   leaves, roughly chopped

This is my favourite lazy weekend eating: spicy, meaty and delicious. Breakfasting on these is a sure-fire way to refuel after a late night. Or cook them on relaxed nights in. They make the perfect throw-it-together supper when the cupboards are bare.

Heat the olive oil in a large heavy-bottomed frying pan and when it is hot, add the onion, chorizo and chillies. Cook for 5 minutes before adding the garlic. Do not allow the onion to burn. If it starts taking colour at the edges, turn the heat down a little. Stir-fry the chorizo mix for about 10 minutes until the onion has turned translucent and the chorizo has released its fat into the pan.

Meanwhile, scoop out the seeds from the tomatoes, dice the remaining flesh and add to the chorizo in the pan. Cook for a few minutes to warm through (you can throw the seeds or use them in a soup or tomato sauce recipe).

Whisk the eggs, milk and cheese together, season with salt and pepper and stir in half the coriander. Add the egg mixture to the sizzling chorizo, turn the heat right up and cook as you like your eggs, runny or set, being wary that they carry on cooking after you have turned the heat off.

Serve scattered with the last of the coriander and, if you can make or get hold of them, fresh corn tortillas (or any other fresh bread).

Chicken & corn humble pie

Feeds 4–6

This is blissfully easy to cook and is a lovely way to use up leftover chicken. You might want to add another chilli when cooking the courgettes, depending on how spicy your tomato sauce is.

Preheat the oven to 180°C/350°F/gas 4. First, get the tomato sauce started so that it is cooking alongside everything else. When it is simmering away gently, take a large heavy-bottomed pan and heat the olive oil and the butter. Add the diced courgette and cook until slightly tender, then add the garlic and the spices and cook for a further 5 minutes. Add the tomato sauce and heat through. Add the chicken, the chopped herbs and season to taste.

To make the corn topping, put the drained corn in a food processor bowl and blend a little. Add the butter, flour and baking powder and whiz again. Season with salt and pepper.

Grease a baking dish with a little butter. Spread half the corn mixture on the bottom of the dish, followed by the chicken and courgette mixture. Scatter the feta on top and then finish with the remaining corn mixture. Bake for 45 minutes until golden and the corn crust is a little firm. This is delicious served with a green salad.

NOTE In the spring, autumn and winter, take out the courgettes and add purple sprouting broccoli, spinach, mushrooms or spring or winter greens instead.

Cooking time:
an hour and a half

500ml Roast tomato sauce
    (see page 30)
2 tablespoons olive oil
30g butter
3 courgettes, roughly diced
2 cloves of garlic
pinch of ground cloves
pinch of ground cumin
pinch of ground cinnamon
300g leftover cooked chicken
    or 2 chicken breasts,
    poached (see page 140)
    and shredded
1 tablespoon tarragon,
    chopped
1 tablespoon parsley, chopped
sea salt and black pepper
500g cooked corn kernels
    (fresh, tinned or from a jar)
55g butter, softened
1 tablespoon polenta or
    plain flour
¾ teaspoon baking powder
60g feta, crumbled

Chilaquiles (the real Mexican nachos)

Serves 4

Cooking time:
40 minutes

2 chicken breasts, poached
(see page 140) and
shredded
1 x Roast tomato sauce
(see page 30)
a small handful of fresh
coriander, roughly chopped
230ml chicken stock
50ml vegetable oil
8 corn tortillas, cut into
triangles
sea salt
2 tablespoons sour cream
grated mature Cheddar,
Parmesan or
Pecorino cheese

Chilaquiles [chee-lah-kee-less] are universally loved by Mexicans. The very thought of them makes our chefs at work go misty-eyed, thinking of home. This is a dish to eat with the family, using up leftover chicken and old tortillas, as classic in Mexico as bubble and squeak is here.

Preheat the oven to 180°C/350°F/gas 4. In a heavy-bottomed pan, mix the shredded chicken, tomato sauce and coriander together. Heat through over a low heat, adding the chicken stock.

Meanwhile, heat the sunflower oil in a separate pan, add the tortillas and when they are crisp, remove and place them on some kitchen paper to remove excess oil. Sprinkle with a little salt.

To assemble the Chilaquiles is rather like a lasagne. Use a large baking dish and start with a layer of tortillas, then a layer of the chicken mixture. Repeat by doing the same for the next layer, and then finish with some sour cream and grated cheese. Bake in the oven for approximately 30 minutes.

Serve with a green salad or some refried beans.

NOTE This is also delicious cooked in the roast salsa verde on page 29.

Fideus seco (spicy crab noodles)

Feeds 6

Cooking time:
about 1 hour

400g vermicelli
   (or angel hair pasta)
100ml olive oil
4 baby shallots, finely
   chopped
4 serrano or other fresh
   green chillies, finely
   chopped
2 x 400g tins plum tomatoes
a good pinch of ground
   allspice
2 tablespoons baby capers
2 bay leaves
sea salt and black pepper
a good pinch of sugar
500ml chicken or fish stock

To serve
300g dressed crab (I love
   Dorset crab towards the
   end of the summer)
4–5 tablespoons sweet
   chipotle paste (see page 38)
lime wedges
a small tub of sour cream
a handful of chopped
   coriander

These noodles are served as a first course in Mexico, rather like pasta in Italy. Smoky, sweet, fiery and flavourful, cook it for people you love.

In a heavy-bottomed frying pan or paella dish, fry the vermicelli in the olive oil, stirring from time to time, for a few minutes until they turn a rich golden colour. Transfer to a sieve, draining the vermicelli on kitchen paper and putting the oil back into the pan.

Over a medium heat, sweat the shallots and chillies for about 10 minutes until the shallots are translucent and starting to break down, and then add the tomatoes, allspice, capers and bay leaves, season with salt, pepper and a good pinch of sugar, and simmer for 15 to 20 minutes whilst you make the chipotle paste and lay the table. Simmering the sauce will concentrate the flavours, giving you a lovely, rich tomato sauce.

Fifteen minutes before you are ready to eat, pour the stock into the tomato sauce, bring to a simmer and cook for 5 minutes over a medium-high heat. Stir the noodles into the sauce and simmer gently until the liquid is absorbed and the noodles are tender.

Serve on plates with the crab, a good spoonful of the chipotle paste on top, wedges of lime, a dollop of sour cream and lots of coriander.

Spicy tomato noodles
For a cheap but deeply comforting, restorative supper dish, leave out the crab and sprinkle the noodles with a little freshly grated Pecorino or Lancashire cheese.

Griddled corn cakes

Makes 6–8 pancakes

Cooking time:
25 minutes

140g plain flour
90g fine polenta
2 tablespoons sugar
½ teaspoon salt
2 teaspoons baking powder
½ teaspoon bicarbonate
    of soda
1 egg
300ml buttermilk
75g butter, melted

There is something incredibly comforting about these
hot corn pancakes. They are delicious sweet or savoury.
I love them with chicken and the mole on page 43.

Sieve the flour, cornmeal, sugar, salt, baking powder
and bicarb into a large mixing bowl and make a well in
the middle. Drop in the egg, whisk in, and then slowly
whisk in the buttermilk. Whisk in all the melted butter,
bar a tablespoon.

Heat a non-stick frying pan until smoking hot, turn down
to a medium-high heat and grease the pan with a drizzle
of melted butter. Add a ladleful of the batter and cook until
bubbles start appearing on the surface. At this stage, flip
the pancake over and cook for a minute or two longer so
that both sides are golden brown. Keep the pancakes hot
in a low oven or plate warmer as you make them.

Serve the corn cakes topped with the grilled prawns on
page 164, mole, cooked chicken or slow-cooked pork or any
of the taco fillings in chapter 5.

NOTE If you can't find buttermilk, add a tablespoon of
lemon juice or white wine vinegar to a jug and fill up with
250ml whole milk. Stir in enough yoghurt to bring the level
up to 300ml and set aside for 5 minutes.

Griddled corn loaf
Bake the batter in a greased loaf or cake tin in a medium
oven (180°C) for about 20 minutes and serve in toasted slices
as above.

Courgette flower omelette with ricotta & tarragon

Cooking time:
30 minutes

4–5 courgette flowers
5 eggs
100ml double cream
50g Parmesan cheese, grated
a small handful of tarragon,
   chopped
sea salt and black pepper
1 tablespoon olive oil
a small knob of butter
½ onion, finely chopped
2 courgettes, diced
   into 1cm cubes
50g ricotta, crumbled

Courgettes are one of the many vegetables that we know and love that were actually first grown in Mexico. Over there, they are so plentiful that their flowers are sold in great big bundles in all the markets and they are eaten in cheesy quesadillas at every other street food stand. They look wonderful laid out on an omelette – it's a beautiful and simple lunch. Just use courgettes if you are struggling to get hold of the flowers.

Preheat your grill to its highest setting. To prepare the courgette flowers, detach the stalks and cube as with the other courgettes. Gently peel back the petals of the courgette flowers and remove the stamen. Tear down one side of a petal so that you can flatten out the flower in a half-moon shape.

Lightly whisk the eggs and cream together, add the Parmesan and chopped tarragon and season well with pepper and a little salt (Parmesan is already pretty salty).

Heat a 26cm frying pan and when it is hot, add the olive oil and butter. When the fat is sizzling, add the onion and courgettes and fry over a medium heat until the onion has turned soft and translucent and the courgette a pale golden colour, but still with a bit of bite. Season lightly with salt and pepper.

Turn the heat right up and when the pan is really hot, pour in the egg mixture, let it cook a little, then drag the mixture from the sides of the pan to the centre with a palette knife. Place the flowers on top in a circular pattern, crumble the ricotta over them and place under the grill. The ricotta will turn a slight golden colour, but the omelette should still be a little wet in the middle. Either serve from the pan or carefully slide on to a large plate. Delicious with crusty bread and a salad.

Spinach & ricotta enchiladas

Serves 4–6

Cooking time:
1 hour

1 quantity of Roast tomato
    sauce (see page 30)
200ml stock
½ teaspoon ground
    cinnamon
sea salt and black pepper
30g pine nuts
olive oil
50g raisins
475g frozen spinach,
    defrosted and drained
½ teaspoon freshly grated
    nutmeg
150g ricotta
6 corn tortillas
4–5 tablespoons sour cream
80g feta, Cheddar or ricotta,
    crumbled or grated

An enchilada is to Mexico what lasagne is to Italy –
designed to make you feel good.

Preheat the oven to 180°C/350°F/gas 4. Heat up the tomato
sauce with the stock and ground cinnamon and check the
seasoning.

Toast the pine nuts in a frying pan and set aside. Add 1
tablespoon of olive oil to the frying pan and add the raisins.
Cook for 2 minutes just until they plump up. Add the drained
spinach, pine nuts, nutmeg, salt and pepper and cook until
the spinach appears dry. Remove from the heat and add
the ricotta.

In a clean frying pan and over a medium heat, warm the
tortillas one at a time in a little olive oil for about 20 seconds
until they become flexible, then quickly drain them on
kitchen paper.

Spoon two tablespoonfuls of the spinach mixture onto the
centre of each tortilla and roll. Cover the base of a 26 x 18cm
ovenproof dish with a few spoonfuls of the tomato sauce and
place the rolled tortillas on top, seam side down. Pour over
the remaining tomato sauce.

Spoon the sour cream on top and sprinkle with the cheese.
Bake for 30 minutes or until the cheese has melted and the
sauce is bubbling.

Chicken and tomato enchiladas
Add the same tomato sauce to leftover chicken to make
chicken and tomato enchiladas.

Mussels linguine with smoky chipotle cream

Feeds 4

I cooked this dish in the semi-finals of Masterchef and I am convinced it helped me to win. This incredibly quick and easy recipe provides a stunningly simple, delicious plate of food. The smoky, sweet heat and creamy, silky sauce is a wonderful foil for the soft spaghetti and mussels.

Cook this in front of your friends to really impress them and get them to help you clean the mussels at the same time! Clean them under a running tap, pulling off the beard between finger and thumb or with a knife (the beard is the bit of tough fibre at the hinge of the mussels). Discard any open mussels that do not close when tapped sharply against the work surface.

Boil a large pan of salted water for the pasta and in a small pan (or microwave) heat the wine until it is warm. Heat the butter and a tablespoon of the olive oil in a heavy-bottomed pan and when the butter is foaming, add the shallots. Turn the heat down to medium so that the shallots do not colour and sweat them for at least 5 minutes until they have softened and turned translucent. Add the garlic, thyme and chipotle purée and cook for a further few minutes. Add the cream, season with salt, pepper and the pinch of sugar and simmer for 5 minutes whilst you cook the pasta and mussels.

Put the pasta on to cook (if you are using dried you will need to cook it for a bit longer). In a large pan big enough to hold the mussels, put the rest of the oil and heat until it is smoking hot. Tip in the cleaned mussels and cover, shaking them over the heat for a minute or two. Add the wine and shake for another few minutes. As they start to open, transfer them to a bowl with a slotted spoon. Discard any unopened mussels. Add the chipotle cream to the mussels.

Drain the pasta when it is al dente and drizzle with a little oil. Strain the mussel juice through a fine sieve into the cream and toss through the pasta. Scatter with chopped coriander and serve the pasta in heated deep bowls.

Cooking time:
20 minutes

1kg mussels in their shells
200ml dry white wine
25g butter
3 tablespoons olive oil
5 shallots, finely chopped
3 cloves of garlic, chopped
the leaves from 4–5
    sprigs of thyme
1 tablespoon Chipotle purée
    (see page 37)
150ml double cream
sea salt and black pepper
a small pinch of caster sugar
350g linguine or spaghetti
    (fresh makes all the
    difference)
a small handful of coriander,
    finely chopped

CHAPTER 10

Puddings

Puddings
are an unadulterated treat in Mexico.

Edible flowers add a delicate, feminine slant to the more macho side of Mexican cookery. The huge variety of fresh fruit means that there is never a shortage of ideas for jellies, ices and compotes. Meanwhile, chocolate – revered in Mexico since the Aztecs – is spiced with cinnamon, allspice or cloves, and sometimes even a touch of chilli.

Churros and flans both come from colonial Spain. The former can be found on street corners across Mexico, whilst flan is sold in almost every cantina. A good flan is hard to resist, especially when it is flavoured with the vanilla beans that have grown throughout Veracruz for hundreds of years. Vanilla makes the most delicious puddings: heated up and infused in creams, chocolate sauces, ice creams and fruit puddings.

The Mexican rice pudding is also a good find, not thick and stodgy as it can be in Britain.

Here then are my favourite guilty pleasures – simple, sensational and sinfully sweet.

Chilli chocolate truffles

Feeds lots

Cooking time:
10 minutes + 1 hour freezing

500g dark chocolate
   (70% cocoa solids)
200g chocolate (at least
   40% cocoa solids)
a good pinch of ground
   cinnamon
2 allspice berries
10 cloves
½ teaspoon chilli flakes
425ml double cream
30g butter
50g cocoa powder

I would recommend doubling or tripling this recipe and storing them in the freezer to pull out in times of need. They make a wonderful end to dinner with a plate of cheese, or a lovely take-home gift for visiting friends.

Grease a baking tin (approx. 30cm by 12cm) with a little vegetable oil and line with clingfilm. Coarsely grate all the chocolate or cut into small uniform pieces, which will make melting the chocolate much easier.

Grind the spices and chillies with a pestle and mortar and heat with the double cream in a heavy-bottomed pan. When hot but not boiling, add to the chocolate in a heatproof bowl and stir in. If you melt the chocolate with cream that is too hot, the chocolate will split, in which case you will need to stir a few tablespoons of cold cream into the melted chocolate. If the chocolate does not melt completely, suspend the bowl over a pan of gently simmering water to warm the chocolate gently. Stir in the butter.

Pour the mixture into the tin, ensuring it is flat and has filled the corners, and freeze for 1 hour. Sieve half the cocoa powder into a large bowl. Turn out the chocolate mixture onto a chopping board and cut into cubes. Toss in the cocoa powder, sieving more over the truffles as you cut them and transfer them to a plastic bag. Store in the fridge or freezer. Devilishly good.

NOTE If you are starting to explore dried chillies, try making these truffles with different varieties and see how the flavours change.

Mexican chocolate sorbet

Feeds 6–8

This sorbet is so silky and rich that it is hard to believe it is not an ice cream. I like to make it for special occasions and pour over the double cream and a generous dash of good quality tequila.

In a medium saucepan, dissolve the sugar, vanilla extract and 550ml water together. Sieve the cocoa powder over the sugar syrup with the cinnamon and salt and whisk briskly to break up any possible lumps of cocoa. Bring the syrup to a low simmer, whisking just until the cocoa powder has been incorporated into the syrup. Turn off the heat and leave to cool for 5 minutes. Now add the chocolate, stirring all the time. If the syrup is too hot, the chocolate will burn and the sorbet will be grainy, so check that the syrup is not scalding hot.

When the chocolate is completely melted, put the pan into a shallow sink full of ice and cold water for about 30 minutes to cool down completely. When it is cool, add the chocolate mixture to your ice cream machine and churn until smooth, thick and starting to set before transferring to the freezer for a final 20 minutes.

Serve the sorbet drizzled with a little (or a lot) of tequila and, if you like, double cream.

Prep time:
45 minutes + churning time

You will need an ice cream machine

200g unrefined caster sugar
½ teaspoon vanilla extract
80g cocoa powder
a few good pinches of
    ground cinnamon
a good pinch of sea salt
180g dark chocolate
    (70% cocoa solids),
    broken up

To serve
100% blue agave tequila
double cream

Vanilla cheesecake with pineapple caramel

Feeds 8–10

Cooking time:
1½ hours

40g butter
140g HobNobs
225g caster sugar
2 tablespoons cornflour
750g cream cheese
6 large eggs, separated
½ teaspoon vanilla extract
150ml double cream
150ml sour cream
pinch of sea salt
zest of 1 lime

For the caramel
a large knob of butter
200g fresh pineapple, peeled,
   cored and chopped into
   small pieces.
a pinch of sea salt
225g caster sugar

This is no ordinary cheesecake. The Mexican cheesecake is light, fluffy and volcanic-looking, cracked across the top to reveal an irresistibly delicate middle. A delicious pudding, with or without the wicked pineapple caramel.

Preheat the oven to 150°C/300°F/gas 2. Lightly grease a 26cm springform cake tin and line the base and sides with baking paper. To make the base, melt the butter and whiz the biscuits in a food processor. Mix together and gently flatten on to the base of the tin. Put in the fridge to chill.

Meanwhile, mix the sugar and cornflour together. Beat in the cream cheese, egg yolks and vanilla extract with an electric whisk. Gradually add the creams, whisking as you do so. Finally add the salt and lime zest.

In a separate bowl, whisk the egg whites to stiff peaks, then fold them carefully into the cheese mixture with a large metal spoon (you want to keep all the air and lightness in the cake). Pour on to the chilled base and bake in the oven for 1 hour 15 minutes, or until the cheesecake is golden on top, trying not to open the oven door! Turn off the oven and leave the cheesecake to completely cool in the oven and only then remove the baking paper.

For the caramel, first melt the butter in a hot pan and fry the pineapple until it is caramelized and golden, seasoning it with the salt and 1 teaspoon of the sugar. Remove from the pan and add the rest of the sugar in its place together with 100ml water. When the sugar has dissolved, turn the heat right up until the sugar has turned a deep, dark golden colour.

Turn the heat down, add another 140ml water, watching for the caramel's spitting, and let it bubble for a few minutes so that the sugar dissolves again and the syrup thickens. Add the pineapple and serve drizzled over the cheesecake or, if it is summer, have the cheesecake with heaps of raspberries.

Mexican flan with tequila syrup

Serves 4

Cooking time:
1 hour, 10 minutes

250g caster sugar
1 tablespoon golden syrup
4 tablespoons reposado
  tequila, warmed
250ml milk
250ml double cream
1 vanilla pod, split
  lengthways down the
  middle
1 whole egg, at room
  temperature
5 egg yolks, at room
  temperature

This is hard to resist, scented as it is with the femme fatale collection of tequila, vanilla and the rich, dark flavours of burnt sugar.

Preheat the oven to 150°C/300°F/gas 2. Pour 100ml water into a pan and add 150g of the sugar and the golden syrup. Turn on the heat, melt the sugar and simmer briskly until the caramel starts to turn a golden colour. Reduce the heat and cook for a further few minutes without stirring, until the sugar turns a deep, dark brown. Carefully add the warmed tequila and spoon the caramel into the bottom of four pudding moulds, being careful to coat the whole bottom by tipping the mould around. Place the moulds in a roasting tin and leave to cool.

Pour the milk and cream into a large pan with the vanilla pod and set over a medium heat. Just before the milk comes to the boil, remove from the heat and cool.

Whisk the egg and the yolks with the remaining 100g of sugar in a bowl and slowly pour in the milk mixture, a little at a time, as you whisk. Once all is combined, return to the pan and place over a low heat. Stir until it is thick enough to coat the back of the spoon.

Ladle the egg mixture into the prepared moulds and fill the roasting tin with hot water, enough to come up near to the top of the moulds.

Bake in the oven for 40 minutes or until the custard is just set. Allow to cool and, when ready to eat, run a knife around the edge of each mould and carefully invert onto a plate.

This pudding is delicious served with quite tart poached fruit.

Salted caramel & nut pancakes

These are quite simply the most delicious, tempting pancakes, attacking all my weak points.

Preheat the oven to 180°C/350°F/gas 4. To make the nuts, start by whisking the egg white until light and frothy. Whisk in the sugar, salt and spices and pour over the nuts, making sure they are thoroughly coated. Bake for 20 to 25 minutes or until they are golden brown, taking care to stir occasionally. When they have cooled, roughly chop and store in an air-tight container (they keep for at least a week so you can make these well ahead).

To make the caramel, put 100ml water with the sugar into a saucepan and place on a medium-high heat. Simmer the syrup, swirling it occasionally until it turns a lovely dark amber colour. Don't stir the caramel with a spoon as it will start to crystalise and form clumps. When your syrup is dark enough, carefully add the Cointreau, cream and orange juice, taking care as the caramel will bubble up furiously. Swirl around on a low heat until all the ingredients have dissolved. A dark (but not burnt!) caramel is key – almost burning the caramel offsets the sweetness, giving a delicious, rich flavour. Season with the salt.

For the pancakes, sift the flour and salt into a food processor with the eggs. Blitz the mix, slowly adding the milk, water and melted butter until you have a smooth batter the consistency of thin cream.

To fry the pancakes, thoroughly heat a non-stick pan, add vegetable oil or a knob of butter and a ladle of batter. As soon as the batter hits the hot pan, tip it around from side to side to get the base evenly coated. It should take only half a minute or so to cook. Flip the pancake and colour the other side – then simply slide it out of the pan and on to a plate. Serve warm with the caramel sauce, scattered nuts and scoops of good vanilla ice-cream.

Feeds 8–10

Cooking time:
an hour

For the nuts
1 egg white
450g walnuts
120g demerara sugar
a few good pinches of
   cayenne pepper
1 teaspoon ground cinnamon
a pinch of ground cloves
2 teaspoons vanilla extract
⅓ teaspoon sea salt

For the caramel
200g sugar
1–2 tablespoons Cointreau
30ml double cream
juice of ½ orange
1 teaspoon sea salt

For the pancakes
110g plain flour
a pinch of salt
2 large eggs
200ml milk, mixed with
   75ml water
50g butter, melted, and more
   for the cooking

a tub of good vanilla
   ice cream

Mango & strawberry salad

Feeds 6

Preparation time:
15 minutes

3 ripe mangoes, (the
   Pakistani honey mangoes
   are delicious)
a large punnet of
   strawberries
1–2 tablespoons unrefined
   caster sugar
juice of 1 lime
a few generous splashes
   of tequila
a large handful of mint
   leaves, roughly chopped

This is a really easy pudding and the richness of the mangoes and the touch of tequila makes it sophisticated enough to impress any dinner guests.

Peel the mangoes, remove the stones and cut the flesh into rough chunks into a salad bowl. Hull the strawberries and cut in half or in thirds if they are very large, adding to the mangoes as you go.

Sprinkle over the sugar, the lime juice and tequila and let sit for at least 10 minutes in the fridge or as long as you want before serving. Bring out before serving to allow the salad to get to room temperature and scatter over the mint leaves.

This looks very pretty served in glass pudding bowls or tumblers.

NOTE Good tequila is delicious in food. Try to get hold of some reposado tequila, which has been rested in barrels for at least 6 months and has a much gentler flavour than younger tequilas.

Old-fashioned vanilla ice

Serves 6

Preparation time:
30 minutes +
24 hours freezing time

1 litre whole milk
2 wide strips of lemon rind
    (use a potato peeler,
    avoiding the pith)
140g sugar
1 vanilla pod, split
    lengthways
1 teaspoon vanilla extract
4cm cinnamon stick
3 egg whites
1 teaspoon lemon juice

An incredibly easy way to make home-made ice-cream, without an ice-cream maker. This pudding takes me back to my very early childhood, when my grandmother would whip up ices like this to beat any shop-bought variety. In Mexico, they are sold all over the place. Magic!

Put the milk, lemon rind, all but 1 tablespoon of the sugar, the vanilla pod, vanilla extract and cinnamon stick into a pan over a low heat and bring to a simmer very slowly. Remove from the heat and allow to cool. Strain the mixture into a freezerproof dish and freeze overnight.

Break the frozen milk up into a food processor and process until it looks a little like slushy snow with no large crystals in it. Return to a large bowl.

In a separate bowl, whisk the egg whites with the remaining sugar to soft peaks and whisk in the lemon juice. Fold 1 tablespoon of whisked egg whites into the frozen milk until smooth, then add the rest. Pour the mixture into the cleaned freezer dish and place in the freezer immediately. Freeze for several hours or overnight until it has the consistency of soft ice cream.

WHY NOT TRY
This is best served when freshly made and is delicious with the poached plums on page 197 or a dollop of the Mexican strawberry jam (see page 203).

Poached plums in rose syrup

Serves 4

I adore plums in any shape or form, but they are particularly exquisite when scented with the petals of wild roses. This is a delicate and lovely late summer pudding.

Place the plums in a shallow, heavy-bottomed saucepan. Dust the icing sugar over the fruit and add 3 tablespoons of water, the rose syrup, lime juice and vanilla pod to the pan.

Put over a low heat and cover with a round of baking paper so that none of the liquid can evaporate. Cook for about 25 minutes until the fruit just holds its shape, but has gone incredibly soft. Do watch the plums like a hawk as they cook quicker than you think and will collapse very easily.

Cooking time:
25 minutes

8 plums, halved and stones removed
1½ heaped tablespoons icing sugar
2 tablespoons rose syrup
juice of ½ lime
1 vanilla pod, split lengthways

Chilled Mexican rice pudding

Serves 6

Cooking time:
40 minutes

200g long-grain rice
1.5 litres semi-skimmed milk
100g caster sugar
a pinch of salt
1 small cinnamon stick,
    broken in half
1 vanilla pod, split in half
    lengthways
rind of 1 orange
rind of 1 lime
3 tablespoons crème fraîche
a sprinkling of ground
    cinnamon

This is a rich, chilled pudding that could grace the smartest
dinner or go down a treat at a children's tea party. Happily,
it can be made well ahead of serving.

Rinse the rice under cold water and drain, then soak for
15 minutes in boiling water. Drain and rinse again.

Put the milk, sugar, salt, cinnamon stick, vanilla pod
(scraping the seeds out first into the milk) and the fruit rinds
into a heavy-bottomed saucepan. Bring slowly to the boil
and once the sugar has dissolved, turn the heat off and allow
the mixture to sit for 10 minutes so the flavours can infuse.

Strain the liquid through a sieve and return the liquid to the
pan with the rice. Bring to the boil, reduce the heat, cover
and gently simmer, stirring every 10 minutes until the rice is
cooked and the mixture has thickened. Remove from the
heat and allow to cool before putting it in the fridge.

After chilling, you will find the mixture has thickened
considerably. Add the crème fraîche and if you prefer a
runnier rice pudding, add a splash of cold milk. Serve
sprinkled with a little cinnamon.

Raspberry & tequila nieve

Serves 4

A nieve is a simple water ice or sorbet. Hugely popular in Mexico, thanks to the hot weather and the enormous range of fruits, they are easy puddings to make ahead of time and are a refreshing end to a summer lunch.

Gently heat 150g of the sugar with 150ml water in a heavy bottomed pan to make a sugar syrup. When the sugar has dissolved, boil for 3 minutes, remove from the heat and set aside.

Purée the raspberries and remaining sugar in a food processor. Pass the purée through a sieve to remove the pips. Add the sugar syrup to the purée, together with the lime juice and only 1 tablespoon of the tequila (too much alcohol will mean that the nieve will never freeze properly).

Pour the mixture into a shallow freezerproof container or tray and place in the freezer for about 2 hours until partially frozen. After 2 hours, remove the nieve from the freezer and mix it up with a fork to break up any ice that is forming. Return to the freezer and leave for another hour. Repeat the process until you have a crunchy frozen nieve.

Serve the nieve in small bowls with a little extra tequila poured on top. I love to serve a scoop of the nieve with a scoop of the vanilla ice on page 196 or little peanut cookies.

NOTE I love to make nieves with whatever berry or fruit is in season. Blackberries are a particular favourite, especially when we have been out picking them in the hedgerows.

Cooking time:
25 minutes

200g caster sugar
500g raspberries
juice of ½ lime
3 tablespoons tequila

Layered passion fruit & flower jellies

Serves 5

Preparation time:
45 minutes +
7–8 hours setting time

For the passion fruit jelly
3 leaves of gelatine
100g sugar
200ml orange juice, strained
100ml passion fruit juice,
    strained
a squeeze of lemon juice,
    if the mixture is too sweet

For the hibiscus jelly
2 leaves of gelatine
85g sugar
5g dried hibiscus flowers
juice of 1 lime
1–2 tablespoons tequila

Jellies are sold in little plastic containers all over Mexico in a wild array of bright colours and patterns. These bright two-tone ones look very fetching and slip down a treat. If you can't get hold of hibiscus flowers, try a berry jelly instead (see below).

First make the passion fruit jelly. Soak the gelatine leaves in cold water until soft. Bring 100ml water and the sugar up to a simmer and simmer just long enough for the sugar to dissolve. Squeeze the gelatine of excess water, drop into the simmering syrup and stir to dissolve. Stir in the orange and passion fruit juices. Cool slightly, pour into five glasses and chill in the fridge for about 4 hours until set.

To make the hibiscus jelly, again soak the gelatine leaves in cold water until soft. Dissolve the sugar in 400ml water over a low heat. Add the hibiscus flowers and simmer for 20 minutes until the flowers have released their colour and flavour. Remove from the heat and strain the liquid. Return to the pan over a low heat, squeeze the gelatine of excess water and add to the simmering hibiscus liquid. Stir to dissolve. Add the lime juice and tequila and cool.

Pour the hibiscus liquid over the passion fruit jelly and return to the fridge. Chill until set.

NOTE There are many different strengths of gelatine, so it's always best to check the suggested quantities on the box.

Passion fruit and blackcurrant layered jelly
Instead of making the hibiscus jelly, cook 150g blackcurrants in the syrup, strain and make as per the instructions for hibiscus jelly.

Fried bananas with a cinnamon sprinkle

Feeds 4

Cooking time:
15 minutes

3 bananas
30g butter
2–3 tablespoons sugar
   (depending how sweet
   your tooth is)
3 tablespoons tequila
2 tablespoons double cream
juice of ½ lime
the merest hint of
   ground cinnamon

I have seen grown men go weak at the knees at the sight of this pudding and once you have tried it you will see why. It is the Mexican equivalent of a good old-fashioned nursery pudding.

Peel the bananas and slice them down the middle so that you have two long half moons. Heat a wide-bottomed frying pan, melt the butter and when it starts to bubble add the bananas, cut side down. Sprinkle with sugar and fry for a minute before turning. Continue frying on a medium heat until the sugar has started to caramelise and the bananas are golden brown.

Pour over the tequila, which may or may not flambée. After 30 seconds, add the cream, lime juice and a tiny sprinkle of cinnamon. A little will add a lovely, mysterious flavour to the bananas, too much will overpower them.

Serve at once with more double cream.

NOTE The quality of the cream really matters here, so try to find farm-fresh, double cream rather than the mass-produced stuff.

Mexican sponge cake with strawberry jam

Serves 10–12

Preheat the oven to 170°C/325°F/gas 3 and grease and flour a 23 x 12cm loaf tin. Place the butter, sugar and vanilla extract in a bowl and, with an electric hand whisk, beat together until light and creamy. It will be ready when it has grown in volume and the butter has turned from yellow to white.

Gradually add the eggs and the clotted cream and beat well. Fold in the flour and baking powder. Spoon the mixture into the loaf tin and bake for 1 hour or until a skewer inserted in the centre comes out clean. Cool in the tin for 10 minutes before turning out onto a wire rack.

While the cake is baking, make the jam. Chill a saucer in the freezer, which will help tell you when the jam is ready. Wash 3 or 4 jam jars in very hot, soapy water, rinse and arrange on a baking tray in the oven to dry out. This process will sterilize the jars.

Lightly wash the strawberries before putting them in a large pan with the sugar and lime juice. Set the pan over a low heat and stir regularly until the sugar has dissolved. Increase the heat to high and bring to a rolling boil. Boil for 4 minutes.

Remove from the heat and drop a little of the liquid on to the chilled saucer and return to the freezer for a minute or two. As it cools a skin will form. If this skin wrinkles when slightly pushed, the jam is ready. If not, return the pan to the heat and boil for a few minutes more, bearing in mind that this jam is meant to be quite runny and that over boiling will mean that you lose the lovely fresh strawberry flavour.

Serve the cake with the jam and a healthy dollop of extra clotted cream on the side, or plain if you prefer.

Cooking time:
1 hour +

185g butter, softened
200g sugar
1 teaspoon vanilla extract
4 eggs
150ml clotted cream
240g plain flour, sifted
1¼ teaspoons baking powder, sifted

For the jam
(makes about 500ml)
500g strawberries
400g preserving sugar
juice of 2 limes

Makes 16 long sticks

Cooking time:
about 1 hour

You will need a piping bag
fitted with a large star-shaped
nozzle

For the churros
90g caster sugar
1 tablespoon ground
   cinnamon
125g plain flour
125g self-raising flour
a good pinch of sea salt
2 tablespoons olive oil
1 litre sunflower oil,
   for frying

For the chocolate sauce
200g dark chocolate
   (70% cocoa solids),
   roughly chopped
50g milk chocolate, roughly
   chopped
2 tablespoons golden syrup
300ml double cream

Churros y chocolate

Devour these plain or stuffed with chocolate sauce – either
way, they are the most decadent thing you could wish for.

Mix the sugar and cinnamon together and set aside.

Make the chocolate sauce. Put all the chocolate in a
heavy-bottomed saucepan with the golden syrup and cream
and heat over a low heat, stirring continuously, to melt the
chocolate, being careful not to let it burn. Alternatively,
heat with short bursts in the microwave, stirring between
each burst.

Sift the flours with a good pinch of salt into a metal or
heatproof bowl and make a well in the centre. In a separate
bowl, mix the olive oil and 450ml boiling water together,
then pour into the well, beating it well with a fork to get rid
of any lumps. The dough should be slightly soft and sticky to
touch. Let it rest for 10 minutes.

Fill a large, heavy-bottomed saucepan with the sunflower
oil – it should be about one-third full. Heat the oil to 170°C or
until a small piece of bread browns in less than 30 seconds.

Add the dough to a piping bag with a star-shaped nozzle
and squeeze out churros directly into the hot oil, cutting
them with a pair of scissors to the length you want. Be
careful not to cook more than 3 at any one time, or they will
all stick together. Fry for about 3 to 4 minutes until crispy and
golden. Remove from the oil with a slotted spoon and drain
on kitchen paper. Sprinkle with the cinnamon sugar.

Reheat the chocolate sauce and pour into little cups for
dipping with the churros.

NOTE These are also good, if thoroughly wicked, to eat for
breakfast with the Mexican hot chocolate on page 218.

CHAPTER II

Drinks

In Mexico, it's common to start the day with
a freshly prepared licuado, a drink of
blitzed exotic fruits and fresh veg, sold in pint
or half-pint measures.

I make these juices regularly at home now. The Vampiro (see page 208) is one of my favourites, with its luminous deep pink colour. Blends of mangoes and oranges are a delight on sunny mornings and the Green goddess juice (see page 208) with fresh apple, parsley and lemon makes me tingle with health. These are really fun to make with kids – you can spray the kitchen with colour knowing the juices are doing them a world of good.

When it is hot and humid outside, I whiz up thirst-quenching Agua frescas, which are fresh, icy waters blended with flowers or fruit and a good dose of sugar or agave syrup. There is no greater way to slake the thirst and they always go down a storm at barbecues and picnics.

After a hard day at work, I am in the mood for stronger pick-me-ups. This might be in the form of a refreshing, soul-affirming Margarita, flavoured with tamarind, hibiscus or just fresh lime. No better drink was designed to get a party going and they saw our wedding night end with dancing until dawn. Over long weekend lunches, I prefer to sip my tequila neat with Sangrita, a wonderful way to enjoy tequila's special flavour that fits right at home with the British taste for Bloody Marys.

When it is cold outside and I am feeling tired and
world-weary, I turn to the intense comfort of a Mexican hot
chocolate, traditionally made with water, not milk,
and lightly spiced with cinnamon. It always hits the spot
– after all, this was the stuff that the Aztec king Moctezuma
drank before going into battle!

Green Goddess fruit juice

Makes 3 glasses

Preparation time: 10 minutes

3 sticks of celery, peeled
    and roughly chopped
4 sweet apples, peeled, cores
    removed and roughly
    chopped
juice of ½ lemon
small handful of mint
small handful of flat-leaf
    parsley

This juice is the most beautiful bright green colour and incredibly fresh tasting. It is a great pick-me-up for when you are feeling tired and low on energy and is supposed to be pretty good for detoxing if you like that sort of thing.

Put the celery, apple and lemon juice into a blender and whiz until completely blended, then add the rest of the ingredients and whiz again. If you have a juicer, just put everything through that.

This juice should be drunk immediately.

Mango, papaya & lime sunshine juice

Makes 4 glasses

Preparation time: 10 minutes

1 ripe mango, peeled and
    roughly chopped
1 papaya (pawpaw), peeled,
    seeds removed and roughly
    chopped
juice of 3 limes
juice of 2 oranges
200ml apple juice

This is delicious, refreshing and tastes of the summer. It is a wonderful way to start the day, or try mixing the juice with prosecco at a party.

Put the first four ingredients into a blender and whiz. Add the apple juice, whiz again and taste. Depending on how sweet the fruit is, you may want to add a little honey or agave syrup. Drink at once.

Jugo de vampiro (vampire juice)

Makes 2 glasses

Preparation time: 10 minutes

2 apples
2 carrots, scrubbed clean
    and topped
2 beetroots, scrubbed clean,
    topped and tailed
juice of 1 lime

A deep, fluorescent pink juice, this is incredibly good for you, both for lowering blood pressure and detoxing.

You will need a proper juicer to make this.

If you have time, place two glasses in the freezer to chill. Cut the fruit and vegetables into rough chunks and push through the feeder of a juicer. Pour the juice into the chilled glasses over ice, if you like, and drink immediately.

Tamarind agua fresca

Makes 3 glasses

Preparation time:
10 minutes

50g tamarind paste
120g caster sugar
juice of 2 limes

Agua frescas are served at every cantina table in Mexico.
They are heaven in hot weather, and make great drinks for
picnics and outdoor barbecues.

Whiz up all the ingredients together in a blender and strain
the mixture through a fine sieve. You may want to add more
lime juice, depending on your taste. Serve with plenty of ice.

Hibiscus agua fresca

Makes a large jugful

Prep time:
30 minutes

60g hibiscus flowers
300g caster sugar
juice of 3 limes
sparkling water (optional)

Dried hibiscus flowers make a delicious tasting drink that
is somewhere between Ribena, cranberry juice and a really
great cocktail.

Put the hibiscus flowers, sugar and 2.5 litres water in a
large pan and bring to the boil. Simmer briskly for about
half an hour to extract the most amount of flavour from the
hibiscus flowers. Strain the flowers through a sieve.
You can add a little caster sugar and red wine vinegar
to the strained flowers and put them in salads or use them to
decorate the glasses.

Add the lime juice to the cordial and taste. You may want
to add a little more sugar. Cool and serve over ice, perhaps
with a little sparkling water to lighten up the flavour.

Cucumber agua fresca

Makes 2 glasses

There is something super refreshing about the light flavour of cucumber. In Los Angeles, one of my favourite cantinas steeps cucumbers in water and serves it to everyone as tap water over ice. This is one of my favourite agua fresca flavours.

Whiz up all the ingredients in a blender with 600ml water and strain through a fine sieve lined with muslin. Serve over ice, sweetening with a little more syrup, if you want to.

Preparation time:
15 minutes

4 English cucumbers
  or 8 short, fat Lebanese
  ones (which have much
  more flavour)
½ serrano or other
  green chilli, chopped
juice of 5 limes
2 tablespoons agave syrup
a pinch of sea salt

Horchata

Makes 4 glasses

Horchata [or-chaa-tah] is like a milky agua fresca made with ground rice and almonds.

Put 1.5 litres water, the cinnamon, almonds and sugar in a large pan and bring the water to the boil. Add the rice and turn the heat down so that the water gets to a gentle simmer. Simmer for 15 minutes before turning off the heat and leaving the mixture to cool. Remove the cinnamon stick. Pour the cooled mixture into a blender and purée. Pour through a fine sieve into a jug and cool.

To serve, pour into glasses filled with ice and dust the horchata lightly with ground cinnamon powder.

Preparation time:
25 minutes

1 cinnamon stick
1 heaped tablespoon
  slivered almonds, toasted
80g demerara sugar
120g long-grain rice

To serve
ground cinnamon (optional)

How to make the perfect margarita

Margaritas are one of my favourite cocktails, mainly because I love tequila and the exhilarating effect it has on me, but also because I love sour cocktails, so anything with plenty of freshly squeezed lemon or lime juice makes me happy. There is a certain ritual to making margaritas for other people because generally everyone likes them served differently. Before you start you need to ask a few questions so that you can make sure you keep everybody happy.

1. Would you like yours straight up, on the rocks or frozen?

Some people like their margaritas blended with lots of crushed ice like a slush puppy. This is a frozen margarita and I think it originates in the US. If your guests like it like this, it means you are going to have to get the blender out. I personally like my margarita on the rocks, which means filling a tumbler completely full with ice, shaking the margarita over more ice, and then straining back into the tumbler. It will absolutely not do to put only a few lumps of ice into a glass because that little amount of ice will melt into the drink, upsetting the balance of tequila to lime to triple sec. Filling it up with masses of ice will keep the drink icy cold and the balance of flavours right. If you are serving a drink straight up, you will win lots of points by keeping a few tumblers in the freezer at the beginning of the night so that the margaritas stay really cold.

2. Would you like a salt rim?

Some people cannot stand salt rims, so it is worth asking this question. If they do want one, run the cut side of a lime along the rim of the glass before filling it with any ice or margarita, and then turn the glass upside down into a saucer of salt. Shake off the excess salt. If you want, you can run the lime along only one half of the rim, which looks pretty and gives people the choice of sipping with or without salt. For those with a sweet tooth, offer to sugar rim the glass for them. Once you have established these two fundamentals, you can make the margarita. There is so much personal choice in margaritas that even from here there is a minefield of decisions. Some people only use Cointreau, which is delicious, if a little expensive, like making a margarita de luxe. It is also delectable with a touch of agave syrup for natural goodness (agave syrup is available from all good health food shops and is an incredibly healthy, slow-release sugar from the agave plant). Some people like their margaritas with sugar syrup, and others prefer without.

Sugar syrup

For a sweeter margarita, dissolve equal quantities of sugar and water, then cool before adding a teaspoon to your cocktail. Keep the syrup in a clean bottle in the fridge – it always comes in handy.

Classic margarita

Per cocktail

Preparation time:
5 minutes

37.5ml 100% blue agave
   tequila
25ml triple sec or Cointreau
12.5ml fresh lime juice
a wedge of lime

Shake all the ingredients over ice and pour into a tumbler.
You may want to add a teaspoon of sugar syrup if you have
a sweet tooth.

Tamarind margarita

Per cocktail

Preparation time:
5 minutes

37.5ml 100% blue agave
   tequila
12.5ml triple sec
   or Cointreau
12.5ml tamarind paste
12.5ml fresh lime juice
10ml sugar syrup
   (see page 210)

I adore a margarita flavoured with the slightly sour taste
of tamarind.

Pour the ingredients into a cocktail shaker and
shake over ice. Pour into a tumbler.

Passion fruit margarita

Per cocktail

Preparation time:
5 minutes

37.5ml 100% blue agave
   tequila
20ml Cointreau
½ passion fruit
12.5ml fresh lime juice

The slightly tart, deliciously fruity flavour of passion fruit is
perfect in a margarita.

Pour the ingredients into a cocktail shaker and
shake over ice. Pour into a tumbler.

Sangrita

Sangrita is a tomato-based drink, very similar to a Virgin Mary. It is flavoured with fresh orange and lime juice, grenadine and masses of Tabasco. This refreshing, spicy, addictive little drink is a fine accompaniment to a good sipping tequila.

Stir all the ingredients together and chill in the fridge. Drink it in small tequila glasses alongside small glasses of tequila or in large tumblers over ice for a spicy version of a Virgin Mary.

Bloody Maria
Serve in a tumbler with a large measure of tequila for a Bloody Maria.

Makes just over 1 litre

Preparation time:
5 minutes

1 litre good-quality
    tomato juice
juice of 2 large oranges
    (you need about 200ml)
juice of 2–3 limes
50ml grenadine
25ml Tabasco sauce
2 tablespoons
    Worcestershire sauce
½ tablespoon sea salt
black pepper

Mexican hot chocolate

Serves 2–4

Cooking time:
10 minutes

100g good-quality
(70% cocoa solids) dark
chocolate, finely chopped
450ml semi-skimmed milk
or water
a cinnamon stick

I adore this drink. When I feel the need for hot chocolate, I don't want a bucket of milk with a slight taste of cocoa, I want intense flavour, energy, and that amazing warm, fuzzy feeling that you only get with really good chocolate.

Put the chocolate into a heat proof bowl. Place the milk or water in a saucepan with the cinnamon stick and, over a low heat, simmer for 2 to 3 minutes. Pour the hot milk over the chopped chocolate and, using a whisk, beat the chocolate until it has dissolved and there is a layer of foam on the surface.

Pour into small cups or bowls and serve immediately. If you are making the hot chocolate with water, you may wish to sweeten it with a little sugar or agave syrup.

Suppliers

Mexican ingredients, from tinned black beans to corn tortillas, and fresh and dried chillies, including ancho, chile de arbol and chipotle, are now available in most large supermarkets, as well as specialist delicatessens across the UK.

If you don't have time to make your own chilli sauces (see Chapter 1), many companies are now making their own for you to try. For sauces made with the delicious smoked jalapeño chilli, or chipotle, look for 'smoky' chilli sauces. Tabasco does a fine smoky version of its classic hot sauce and the Cool Chile Company and others sell chipotles 'en adobo' to add to your cooking. You can find some wonderful sauces containing a whole range of other chillies, from habanero to ancho and pasilla, so experiment with the flavours you like best.

If you want to adventure deep into the heart of this cuisine, it's never been easier to find authentic Mexican ingredients online. Some farmers (see below) are now growing fresh poblano chillies, that look like a green pepper, and fresh tomatillos, which are related to the cape gooseberry and taste bright, citrusy and delicious. Also, look out for herbs like dried epazote and Mexican oregano and the famous Yucatan seasoning achiote. I do an Internet shop every few months, as Mexican chillies and spices last for ages in the cupboard.

Brindisa, a Spanish stockist, sells ñora chillies, guindillas, choriceros and sweet and spicy smoked paprika, which can be used to replace ancho chillies in recipes.
www.brindisa.co.uk

Bristol Sweet Mart offers a range of dried chillies, plus tortillas, Mexican chocolate, pickled jalapenõs, black beans, refried beans and much more.

80 St Marks Road
Bristol BS5 6JH
0117 9512257
http://www.sweetmart.co.uk

Find a rich variety of dried chillies (ancho, chipotle, tins, arbol, pasillo, mulatto) at **Casa Mexico**, plus dried oregano, jalapenõs, black beans, tortillas, salsas, and much more.

1 Winkley Street,
Bethnal Green,
London E2 6PY
Tel: 0207 739 9349
http://www.casamexico.co.uk

Chilli Lime Deli stocks a range of spices, hot sauces, beans and jalapenõs, available both in-store and to order online.

Chilli Lime Deli
17 Fleming Square
Blackburn
Lancashire BB2 2DG
Tel: 01254 52229
www.chillilimedeli.co.uk

The Cool Chile Company was one of the first places in the UK to sell Mexican chillies, herbs and spices as well as a very good corn flour and tamale flour for making Mexican streetfood. Their restaurant, the Taqueria,

sells everything too, as does their stall at Borough Market.

Taqueria
139-143 Westbourne Grove
London W11 2RS
Tel: 0207 229 4734
www.coolchile.co.uk

For the hottest chillies and an impressive range of home-made chilli sauces, **Chilli Pepper Pete** is a great place to shop.
www.chillipepperpete.com

Edible Ornamentals was the first British farm to do pick-your-own chillies and also sells a range of fresh and dried products.

Edible Ornamentals
Cherwood Nursery
Blue Bells
Chawston

Bedfordshire MK44 3BL
Tel: 01480 405 663
www.edibleornamentals.co.uk

Lupe Pinto's Deli has
outlets in both Edinburgh and
Glasgow, as well as an
online shop featuring a range
of imported Mexican sauces
and groceries, herbs and
spices.

Lupe Pinto's Deli
311 Great Western Road
Glasgow, G4 9HR
Tel: 0141 334 5444

Lupe Pinto's Deli
24 Leven Street
Edinburgh, EH3 9LJ
Tel: 0131 228 6241
www.lupepintos.com

MexGrocer stocks everything
from masa harina flour to an
inexpensive tortilla press.
www.mexgrocer.co.uk

Peppers by Post are based in
Dorset and created the
hottest chilli in Britain, the
Dorset Naga. Find chillies,
Mexican herbs and tomatillos
here, in season.

Peppers by Post
Michael and Joy Michaud
Sea Spring Farm
West Bexington
Dorchester
Dorset DT2 9DD
Tel: 01308 897 766
www.peppersbypost.biz

South Devon Chilli Farm is
an amazing resource of fresh
chillies, dried chillies, chilli
sauces, chilli chocolates and
chilli jellies.

South Devon Chilli Farm
Wigford Cross
Loddiswell
Kingsbridge
Devon TQ7 4DX
Tel: 01548 550 782
www.southdevonchillifarm.
co.uk

The Spice Shop in London
is worth a visit, for its wide
selection of Mexican chillies,
both fresh and dried but
beware, its prices are out of
this world!

The Spice Shop
Blenheim Crescent
London W11 2EE
Tel: 0207 221 4448
www.thespiceshop.co.uk

Wally's Delicatessen in Wales
stock a selection of chillies,
pickled jalapenos, cooking
chorizo and cider vinegar.

Wally's Delicatessen
42–44 Royal Arcade
Cardiff
South Glamorgan
CF10 2AE
Tel: 029 20229265

World of Chillies is a small,
family-run business in
Manchester, which offers you
the chance to grow your own
chillies from seed, as well as
a variety of fresh and dried
chillies to capture the
imagination.

World of Chillies
44 Windsor Road
Levenshulme
Manchester
M19 2EB
0161 2253114
www.worldofchillies.com

If you are still in doubt perhaps
you should be heading to the
annual chilli festival at the
gardens of West Dean, Sussex
in August to see what's
growing in the UK.

www.westdean.org.uk

Index

Page references for illustrations are in *italics*

Tell Me What You Think

I'd love to know how you get
on with the food and techniques
in this book. Got a practical
suggestion you'd like to make,
an update on chilli suppliers to
share, or a query about one of
the dishes? Please write to me
at www.thomasinamiers.com or
twitter.com/thomasinamiers.

Tommi x

Acknowledgements

Not being Mexican, but having fallen in love with the country's food, I constantly feel a debt of gratitude to this beautiful country and to a host of Mexican chefs, writers and friends who have helped me on my journey of discovery and always made me feel at home.

Thank you to Alicia Gironella, for the many delicious meals at El Tajin with Giorgio; to Carmen Titita Ramirez of El Bajio who sent me to Veracruz armed with the best food addresses; to Roberto Solis from Nectar in Merida for unceasing enthusiasm and advice; to Alejandro Ruiz from Casa Oaxaca and his magical, locally-inspired cooking (see his influence on page 136); to Patricia Quintana, Monica Patiño and Enrique Olvera in Mexico City and to Josefina Santacruz in New York.

Thank you to Sam Hart for sending me to Mexico in the first place and to Sam Carter, Damian Fraser and Alex Garcia Ponce who were the kindest and most supportive of friends during my time there and since; also to Sophie, Crispin, Tim, Rawds, Paloma and all the Holmes – you are all a big part of this book. Also a big thank you to all the published Mexican food writers who allowed me to continue my journey from my kitchen back at home.

I would like to thank the inimitable Diana Kennedy. To this day I do not know if my hero worship was influenced by our common nationality but your writing constantly informs my Mexican cooking and your spirit inspires me to live more vividly, courageously and adventurously. Many thanks for the recipes on page 33 and page 42.

At home I thank my agent Antony Topping, who has been gently and patiently pushing me to write this book for some years now. To Emma Miller, for her tireless support in the kitchen; to the Mexican Tourist Board for help on finding amazing places to visit in Mexico and to Daniel Dultzin whose boundless love for Mexico has inspired me since we first met.

To my editor Zelda Turner, who has coped with my sometimes distracting passion for all things Mexican and somehow teased out a coherent book from me. To Kay Halsey, Sarah Hammond, Alice Wright, Camilla Dowse, Emma Knight and everyone at Hodder for all their hard work and enthusiasm for this book. And to Tara Fisher, Wei Tang and Ami Smithson for the beautiful photography, styling and design.

Thank you to all of you at Wahaca for such an incredible ride over the last four years, in particular to the patience and good humour of Mark and Carolyn, Arturo and Harish; and to my friends who stick by me through thick and thin. To my family who have never ceased to be critical but largely appreciative guinea pigs during endless recipe testing; to WOLF and SUB-Zero for providing me with the most incredible kitchen kit and to my genius father for designing around it the most beautiful kitchen anyone could wish for.

Most of all to my husband, Mark, whose unstinting enthusiasm, loyalty and belief buoys me through all things.